I0404885

Take Off Your Glasses

Fernando Lanzer

Published with the support of
LCO Partners BV
Meester F. A. van Hallweg 23
1181ZT – Amstelveen
The Netherlands

First printing September 2012

ISBN-10: 1480054771
ISBN-13: 978-1480054776

Cover design & photography by Bruna Pereira de Souza

Back cover photo by Jussara Pereira de Souza

Praise for "Take Off Your Glasses"

"I find the book "Take Off Your Glasses" excellent, maybe the best common language explanation of my ideas that has been written so far."

Professor Geert Hofstede (University of Maastricht, Netherlands)

"I think it is a great book, you are different because you really say what needs to be said. Many people are simply afraid to "rock the boat", especially here in the US, and this is why so many social and cultural fallacies keep being promoted and validated. I like very much the chapter The United States of Europe and the American Union."

Cosmin Gheorghe (Synergis Counseling, Coaching & Consulting, USA)

"Thank you for passing this on. "Democracy in China" is the best article I have ever seen on Power Distance and clarified things for me too. I have lived in several countries with high Power Distance and found that this article summarized very well the attitudes of the citizens of these countries.

I agree with you that it is a timely reminder that we should be very wary of value judgments and there may be no such thing as "good" or "bad" on the culture scales, only "different". It is however extremely hard to reach this level of detachment, even when one understands the two cultures very well: we are all prisoners of our own cultural upbringing and education!"

Marvin Faure (Mindstore, Switzerland)

Thank you for sending this, and I do really like it. It is the best (concise, clear, drily amusing) summary of Power Distance I have come across. I hope you don't mind, but I'm forwarding it on to people I know who are working with their clients on issues resulting from different perceptions of Power Distance.

Michael Newman (Enablers Network, UK)

"By the way, I read and enjoyed your article on Democracy in China. It makes a lot of sense. I never saw things from the high/low PDI perspective. After living 30 years in Venezuela and observing the situation now, I can definitely see how ones culture and PDI have an impact on everything."

David Charner (ERC Consultants, USA & Venezuela)

"I read this with interest when you first sent it (and since visited China where I saw this at first hand!). However, it is all the more interesting now because I am in (southern) Italy running a course for 21 Mediterranean students from Syria, Egypt, Tunisia, Jordan, Iraq, Algeria and Palestine. The PDI concept within the current context of the Arab world is playing out in front of me every day with young, intelligent and engaging students. So too is it when I return to my room and watch BBC, Aljazeera, Press TV and CCTV. In all of these outlets it strikes me that the BBC has lost touch with the new reality as perhaps has the West in general. Thanks for sending me this excellent piece."

Sayed Azam-Ali (University of Nottingham, Malaysia Campus)

"Coming from Hong Kong, in spite of all the liberties I enjoy, I echo that power, privilege and responsibility are attached to positions. And I personally believe that it should stay this way here. In fact, I think that high power distance works better with capitalism given its meritocratic nature."

Victor Wong (AIESEC Hong Kong)

"Thank you very much for sharing your article. It is very interesting and I agree with your insights. The democracy is differently working in China and it is working very well. The collective leadership in China has well planned succession plan and it works smoothly. They don't spend huge time and money for elections. Only one party dominates the politics, but they have pretty good plans to develop economy and society. There will be some mistakes and oppressing different opinions but they at least improved life of people significantly so far. I think they set up a good model for developing countries.
So, I realized later that different culture in developing countries will need different democracy system from western countries."

K. R. Yoon (Du Pont, South Korea)

Thanks for the book! I had a good laugh about Master Khard quoting the Beatles.

Geert Jan Hofstede (Author, "Exploring Culture", Netherlands)

To my

Wife, who inspired me to write

Parents, who inspired me to publish

Children, who taught me to live

Bosses, who developed my patience

Clients, who gave me joy

Table of Contents

Preface

These stories have been written as comments on issues happening around us. When I say "issues" I mean things that are relevant to people who have some awareness of the world existing beyond their neighborhood, the town they live in, the country in which they currently live, the cultures in which they have been brought up.

When I say "us", I mean people who share an interest for such issues: they are sometimes about politics, often about culture, always about life.

I hope you enjoy reading them and that they provoke some emotion in you: joy, contempt, happiness, anger... I also hope to provoke some reflection, curiosity, perhaps a desire to do something about what is important to you: whether it is playing with your children or protesting on the streets, being a better manager or increasing your professionalism. Thinking and feeling are important, but believing and acting upon your beliefs, thoughts and feelings is what helps make this world a better place.

Ultimately, that's why I wrote these stories: to share them with you hoping they will add some value. Perhaps the value-added will be just a smile, now and then—that is actually something we could all use more of!

1. Take Off Your Glasses

We all develop since early childhood a "culture bias": what we perceive as similar to our own culture values, we consider to be "good" or "right". Whatever we perceive to be different from our own culture values, we consider being "bad" or "wrong".

We look at the world through colored spectacles or sunglasses, which distort our perception. We see everything through these tinted sunglasses, and each culture has its own biased vision, shared by members of that culture. This has been demonstrated repeatedly in research, it's not just some "pipe dream" or somebody's opinion.

In order to understand the world outside of your own culture, you first need to be aware of your own culture bias. You first need to be aware of your glasses and take them off, in order to see other cultures as they really are.

Media content generators in the English language are largely wearing "Contest" culture glasses. This means that the main providers of news on a global scale (CNN, BBC, Fox, Sky, NYT, FT, Economist and others) are wearing tinted glasses and we should all be aware of that. Let's take a look at the glasses they are wearing and what the world would look like if these glasses were removed.

"Contest" Culture Glasses

Hofstede's 5D model revealed in research that the Anglo-Saxon culture ("Contest") is egalitarian, individualistic, performance-oriented, relatively comfortable with ambiguity, and it is normative. Knowing this allows us to see the type of glasses usually worn by people from this culture. The glasses they wear affect their perception, thus affecting the content they generate and disseminate in the media. Here are some typical issues that get distorted and/or overblown by “Contest” culture glass-wearers.

Privacy

We see in the media (TV, internet, newspapers, magazines) that “privacy” is a big issue. People are worried about surveillance cameras, phone hacking, identity cards, because these things represent a threat to privacy. They constitute potential invasions of privacy, and that’s a big thing.

Well, actually, it’s not... Or, rather, it is an issue indeed in the “Contest” culture and also in all “individualistic” cultures. However, these cultures account for less than 15% of the world’s population. This means that 85% of the people on the planet are not really that much into the whole “privacy” thing. I’m not saying that invasion of privacy is not an issue; I’m just saying it is not such a BIG issue as you would be led to believe from what you see in the media.

When the BBC reports on “invasion of privacy” being a major concern in the Middle East or in Asia, they are actually talking about the BBC’s (English) bias when looking at what is happening there. The reporter’s outrage may be genuine, but it is not necessarily the outrage of the people who are affected by happenings in that location. It’s in the eyes of the beholders, and if the beholders are all wearing tinted glasses (also people watching in London and New York), the picture being painted will seem real to all of them, but not to the subjects being portrayed.

People in “collectivistic” cultures are not that worried about privacy; they will easily share details of their lives with complete strangers, something unthinkable to members of an individualistic culture. The reaction of “individualists” to such sharing is often “Whoa! Too much information! I don’t need to hear that!” To collectivists, they are just trying to be friendly, and the negative reaction is perceived as “rude” and “cold”.

So, if you are part of a “Contest” culture or any other individualistic culture, please remove your glasses before getting riled up on privacy issues outside your own culture. For most people on the planet, it’s not THAT important. They are more concerned with gaining intimacy rather than protecting their privacy.

Polarization

This gives the expression "polarized glasses" a different meaning... In a "Contest" culture there is a tendency towards seeing two opposing forces confronting each other. Issues are easily seen as "bi-polar", that is: there is always a thesis and always an antithesis opposing it. In such cultures there is less value ascribed to multilateral thinking: the coexistence of many different forces or opinions regarding a certain issue. The "Contest" culture generates typical expressions such as: "you are either with us, or against us", "it is 'us' versus 'them'", and "there are two kinds of people in the world".

This leads to a certain oversimplification of complex issues. The situation in Europe is a good example of such a complex issue, which is usually oversimplified by American and English media reporting on it. To the UK and US, European leaders are incompetent because they are unable to decide between two options when confronting issues. Leaders in Europe look at situations and see many different options, equally important, rather than a confrontation between "A" and "B". By definition, a multilateral perspective is more complex than a bi-lateral one, so it is no surprise that discussions take longer and a conclusion is difficult to reach. Alliances are necessary, and these require time, plus they may add to the complexity.

The "polarized distortion" applies to other issues in other parts of the world, as well. The "Contest" culture sees two opposites everywhere: it's "the haves versus the have-nots", the "capitalists versus the communists", "New School versus Old School", "macho versus feminists", etc. In other cultures, such as the Dutch and Scandinavians, or the Latin Americans, or the Africans, the same situations are viewed as "multilateral".

This difference is very evident in politics: while "Contest" cultures are typically "bi-partisan", other cultures have many equally relevant parties and need coalitions to govern. It is less evident but equally true in other aspects of life. For instance, gender issues are not "just" about men and women, but they are also about gays, and lesbians, and people who are gay-lesbian sympathizers, and people who think gender equality actually depends on age, or on the nature of the role, or who consider sexual preference as different from gender, and so on. Religion is not viewed as "Christians versus

Muslims", but rather as the many Christian and Islamic sects, plus the Buddhists, Hindu and others still.

Meritocracy

Management textbooks seem to take meritocracy as a given, but we tend to forget that the majority of them are produced in "Contest" cultures, which are clearly performance-oriented. Cultures that are more "caring-oriented" and "quality-of-life" oriented will pay lip service to meritocracy (to comply with the textbooks) but will act very differently in practice.

In practice, in these cultures meritocracy is "de facto" trumped by caring. People get promoted because they have been longer with the firm, or because they belong to an influential family, or because they went to a renowned business school. People from the "Contest" cultures will look at these situations and express outrage. They will think that "the locals" share their outrage. In practice, "the locals" will also express outrage when they are on the losing end of a decision, but will typically decide according to the same criteria they criticize, when put in a deciding position in a similar situation. Don't be so quick in promoting meritocracy and deriding other approaches—look at the context first, take off your glasses and then try to see what would be best in a certain situation.

Urgency

In "Contest" cultures speed is valued: acting fast, deciding quickly. There is usually a great sense of urgency, time is of the essence. When decisions take a bit longer, people get anxious. When looking at decision-making processes in other cultures, often "Contest" people are irritated when things do not happen as quickly as they would like to see them happen. The concept of "time is money" is deeply ingrained in a culture that is performance-oriented, and performance can be easily appraised by measuring time spent and the amount of money made.

Yet, in "Network" cultures such as the Dutch and the Scandinavian, urgency is trumped by other factors: making sure that all stakeholders are included and heard is more important than making decisions quickly. Deadlines are often not met, but this is not important, if missing the deadlines was necessary to ensure quality of output or satisfaction of stakeholders.

"Contest" culture media will typically report that missing a deadline or delaying a decision are signs of failure (refer to discussions on the Euro zone). Yet the people involved, if they are members of a "Network" culture, will not consider this necessarily as a problem. They may simply think that stakeholder satisfaction is more important than deadlines. What is portrayed as failure in one culture may be portrayed as success in another.

Women's Rights

The "Contest" media is filled with items about women's rights. It seems, sometimes, that the only reason for NATO to be in Afghanistan is because of women's rights. Yet the issues of gender equality most often are seen from a different perspective by women from other cultures. I've always found it amusing that some cultures look at the US and see it as a matriarchy, a culture in which women dominate men... To an American feminist this seems to be utter nonsense, but we all need to take off our glasses and look at cultures more objectively.

Since "Contest" cultures are performance oriented, caring for the family is seen as less important, it is less valued. Family reunions such as Thanksgiving are often portrayed as unpleasant affairs. Feminists fight for equality in the workplace, because work is more valued than quality of life.

In some other cultures, quality of life is more valued than performance. Women are less interested in work, and men are also less interested in work. Gender equality discussions focus on asking men to be more active in taking care of the family and doing home chores; they are asked to be more "caring-oriented", rather than to support equal pay at work.

I was pleased to read that a woman in Libya rejoiced at the downfall of Colonel Kaddafi, because he had forbidden the wearing of bhurkas. Now this woman was celebrating the fact that she could wear a bhurka, like she wanted...

"Contest" culture feminists tend to think that women all over the world share the same struggle for equality. Actually, gender equality has different meanings and connotations in different cultures, and these need to be considered carefully. Depending on the culture, the objective of gender equality will be reached through shifts in the roles of both men and women, in ways that are consistent with that culture. Women's ambitions also may be different from one culture to another.

Democratization

Churchill once said, "Democracy is the worst form of government, except for all those other forms that have been tried." This, of course, is a very Anglo-Saxon point of view, and as such it has been often repeated and amplified in the Anglo-Saxon media. People from other cultures may also take a similar view, especially if they are coming from an egalitarian society. However, the same is not true in hierarchical societies, in which many people take the view that a form of "enlightened despotism" is preferable to democracy.

This is considered totally undesirable in a "Contest" culture. People from "Contest" cultures tend to misinterpret protests against government in hierarchical societies. They tend to see them as movements demanding democracy, when actually most of the times these protests demand simply the replacement of government by someone who will do a better job of running the country.

There are more than enough examples of this, the most blatant ones to be seen in Russia and China, both hierarchical societies. In both countries there was a long history of despotism, for centuries. In both countries, the despots were overthrown and replaced by communist regimes, in the 20th century. The communist leaders proceeded to lead with as much authoritarianism as their predecessors, with support from the majority of the population.

In both countries, again, there was a point in time in which the communist regimes were challenged. In Russia it was replaced by a capitalist republic, yet the same ruler has led the country for almost 20 years with an authoritarian style (and the support of the majority). In China the economy is becoming capitalist, while the political regime is authoritarian communism. In both cases, a form of democratization may be happening, but in a way not at all similar to what is seen in the US or the UK. Democratization, if it happens at all, will take a very different shape in each country, according to the respective culture.

Research has shown that it is people who "make" dictators. A hierarchical culture will generate strong rulers with absolute power, regardless of the political regime. An egalitarian culture will generate rulers who are less authoritarian, because authoritarianism is not accepted.

"Contest" culture people look at hierarchical societies and see people who are oppressed by force and who are yearning for democracy. The reality is, the ruler can only keep himself/herself in power with support from the people. As soon as that support is lost, dictators are overthrown, and replaced by another strong ruler. Every dictator has support from a large part of the population, most often by the majority. "Contest" culture people may find dictators despicable, but in hierarchical societies most people feel that strong rulers are needed to maintain order. They just want a strong ruler that is also inspiring and effective.

Equality

Underlying the concept of democracy is the concept of equality, the idea that all people are equal and should have the same amount of power in society. "Contest" cultures hinge on the notion that life is a competition, but all people should have an equal opportunity to "win" this competition through their performance and fair play on a level playing field. Any idea straying from this notion is extremely annoying to "Contest" culture individuals.

However, Hofstede's research revealed that only 9% of the world's population lives in "egalitarian" cultures (basically the Anglo-Saxons, Germanics (includes Swiss, Austrians) and Dutch-Scandinavians). Everybody else lives in hierarchical societies. In these societies, people consider that there is an unequal distribution of power in any community, no matter how large or how small, and that this is just a fact of life. It is a reality to be accepted.

This doesn't mean that people like it; it just means that they consider it unavoidable. Therefore, many focus on making their way to the top of the pecking order. They may oppose the current rulers or bosses, but once they are able to replace the incumbents, they will exercise power in a very similar way and maintain its unequal distribution.

It's a mistake to think that people from hierarchical cultures have a desire for equality; more often then not, they are simply striving to improve their own position in the hierarchy.

Supremacy Of Reason

In "Contest" cultures there is a notion that people should be rational, and that emotions are a "lesser" aspect of human beings. Emotions interfere with the efficiency and effectiveness of making rational decisions, therefore they should be suppressed. Values are seen as a "fluffy" subject, in conflict with the pragmatic aspects of life. Discussing values simply delays concrete action, so such discussions should be avoided or kept out of the way.

In other cultures, such as in Latin America and the Middle East, emotions are equally important as reason, if not more. Decisions are often taken due to emotional motives. People are often admired for doing that, rather than for "keeping their cool". Being "hot blooded" is regarded as a positive quality, rather than a weakness. When the "Contest" culture media criticizes someone for "being emotional", they should realize that in many parts of the world such behavior is encouraged and praised, rather than punished.

As for the values discussions, pragmatism often is used as a justification for unethical behavior. The need for acting swiftly should not be such that it means choosing for rapid action that is unethical, rather than carefully considering ethical implications before deciding on action.

The financial mess that happened in 2008 was brought about precisely for looking at "rational" business issues and not looking at ethics, nor at the emotional basis and consequences of economic behavior. Cultures which put reason in perspective and which regard it as just as important as, but not more important than, emotions and values, may be in a better position to cope with the complex issues we all need to face in the 21st Century. Being comfortable with emotions and values is just as important as being comfortable with rational analysis.

Wear Sunscreen, But Take Off Your Glasses

Years ago an article by Mary Schmich went viral. It dispensed many life lessons and pearls of wisdom, but the main advice was... "wearing sunscreen", repeated several times. Here we emphasize not sunscreen, but tinted glasses; and we don't recommend wearing them, but rather taking them off... Wearing "Contact" culture glasses all the time leads to serious misinterpretations about what is really going on in the world outside the Anglo-Saxon culture. Wearing tinted culture glasses does not improve your vision, it distorts it.

This, of course, is an issue not only in Anglo-Saxon cultures, but also in any culture. In order to improve cross-cultural understanding, the first thing we must all do is take off our glasses. In other texts, we will look at the glasses worn by people from other cultures.

2. Managing People Across Cultures

Managers all over the world, we are in for a tough time during the global economy's first truly global downturn. Managing in a global marketplace is already quite a challenge for most of us. Managing during a global downturn is twice as challenging. For the first time we are experiencing the true interdependence of markets all over the world, in every sense. People have been talking about a "flat world", a "global economy" and similar notions for more than a decade, but it is during our first truly global recession (or is it already a global depression?...) that these interdependencies become painfully evident. The crisis in the financial markets spread out all over the world in a matter of days and spilled onto the consumer markets, the labor markets, the production cycles of just about every industry you can think of, and are affecting everyone from Arkansas to Abu Dhabi, from Zagreb to Zimbabwe, and every place in between.

The challenges managers face have gained in complexity, because operating in global interdependent markets means operating in a series of hugely diverse landscapes. Globalization does not equal standardization, but rather it means selling to very different people in different parts of the world, and managing very different people in the production and distribution cycles needed to deliver all over the world.

The essence of a manager's main challenge, however, remains the same: it is to manage people effectively. Managing people is the main job of any manager. Some would argue that managing people is the **only** job of any manager. And the main difficulty of that job starts with denial. Many managers are still under the illusion that managing people is not their main job, that it is someone else's responsibility ("Those idiots in HR are supposed to do this! I'm too busy managing the business!").

Well, I'm sorry to disturb you and wake you up from your cozy escapist dream, but reality is that managing people is not what HR is supposed to do, it's what you, the manager, must do. The guys in HR are supposed to assist you by providing guidelines and tools and learning opportunities to help you face that challenge. Hiding under the bed won't help you face the challenge.

I know it's a difficult job, handling people, much more difficult for most people than figuring out those complex mathematical equations involved in rocket science, much more difficult than brain surgery and other technical challenges that we all read about as the biggest challenges of our civilization. I'm not saying rocket science is easy. I'm just saying that managing people, in practice, is more difficult, because it requires both rational AND emotional skills. It requires IQ and EQ. And most of us have been (wrongly) educated to believe that rationality is what you really need to be successful. It's not. For that (the rational aspects of work), we have robots, and computers, and IT consultants from the 90's. But to make it all come together effectively, we need people and effective managers with IQ and EQ. So let's look at what managers can do to become better at managing people.

And as we start, let's look at another scary issue that sends managers scurrying back to hide under the bed of denial again, just as they were mustering the nerve to come out and face the music: cultural diversity. ("Aw, c'mon! It's bad enough that you say we have to manage people and try to grasp all those fuzzy emotional things that no one can calculate or measure, now you're going to tell us that people are totally different from each other and that they have different notions of what is right and wrong depending on where they come from? How am I supposed to get things done the right way if people don't agree with what is "right"?").

Yeah, I know I'm being a pain in your assets (specially hurts during a financial crisis), but if you don't come out from under that second bed, it'll only take longer to sort this whole thing out and fix the global economy. You can have your dessert afterwards.

So, let's look at how we can manage very different people, from different cultures, all over the world, and get the global economy going again by being more effective and more efficient.

Managing people is not easy, but it's simple

Many things in life are difficult to do, but they are actually simple to figure out. We have a tendency to over-complicate stuff. It makes us feel proud when we can solve an apparently complex issue. So we tend to take simple issues and describe them in a complicated way. By doing this, we can pose as "experts" when we solve seemingly unsolvable problems. Thus lies the challenge of keeping simple things simple. We must avoid the temptation to complicate them. We must focus on doing the simple stuff that is necessary to be done, and avoid the long, complicated discussion around the issue, which is actually a way of avoiding getting down to action. The simple stuff that needs to be done is also often scary stuff, which we would rather not face. Hence complication is a form of avoiding the simple essence. Complication is a form of using rationality as a shield to defend ourselves from the emotional consequences of acting.

So, back to doing the simple stuff. Managing people is actually about carrying out five steps in a process and repeating them over and over again. Hopefully, getting better at it each time you repeat. We hopefully learn from experience, we adapt and improve continuously. I like to think of the five steps in an acronym: R-STAR.

These are the "R-STAR" steps in the cycle of managing people:

1. Recruiting (getting the people you need, to get started).
2. Setting targets (or agreeing what people need to do)
3. Training (or teaching people how to do what they need to get done)
4. Appraising (providing feedback on work progress, correcting direction, etc.)
5. Rewarding (providing consequences, good or bad, to reinforce desired behavior and avoid repetition of undesired behavior)

Doesn't look like rocket science, does it? But it's so much more difficult than rocket science... Remember, the difficulty lies in keeping it simple!

The "complication committee" that lurks in every organization would quickly point out that things are much more complex than that five-point sequence. They would also point out that things actually start earlier than that, when things like "what actually needs to be done" are defined and decided upon. It's okay; I can go along with that and still keep it simple. Let's go to "The Beginning".

"In the beginning"... there was nothing, and then a Client came along and expressed a Need (directly or indirectly). Some people say that "The Client is King!" I like to think that "The Client is God!" in the sense that the Client is the beginning and the end of everything. Please excuse the blasphemy, forgive my sins and bear with me for a while.

As the Client expresses a Need, the entrepreneur steps forward to satisfy that need, and organizes a company to satisfy that need. This can be a one-man show, in which case the entrepreneur is just managing himself (the "R-STAR" cycle still applies, but that's another article, let's not go there now), or any size of organization, from two people to two hundred thousand people, and every size of group in between. The organization (let's assume a company of up to around a hundred people, which represents most of the companies around the world) makes plans to carry out the actions necessary to satisfy that Client Need, organizes work, distributes roles, and it boils down again to several managers within the company, each being charged with something that needs to be done, for which they need to get the people and do it, by going through the "R-STAR" cycle.

The result of each "R-STAR" cycle is a product or service (or part thereof) that serves the ultimate purpose of satisfying that Client Need. Client Satisfaction is the end of the cycle. The circle is complete. If you want, you can add to the acronym and call it "Clients R-STAR-S", in which the last "S" stands for "Satisfaction".

Of course, every step in the cycle actually hides a whole universe of stuff, and we all enjoy playing around with it a lot, so much so that we often lose sight of the "Whole" and forget how what we are immersed in actually links with everything else and provides a sense of purpose to what we do in our lives. By the way, "Humankind" is the ultimate Client, and everything we do serves the ultimate purpose of making this a better world for Humankind and the next generations, but that's another article, so let's not go there either, for now.

Let's stick with the simple and difficult task of managing people and carrying out the "R-STAR" cycle. Let's briefly look at each of the five steps.

Recruiting can be subdivided into many interlinked aspects, highly sophisticated when you're talking about a multinational organization operating in 20 countries or more. You've got "Positioning" of your "Employer Brand", you've got all kinds of "Recruiting Strategies" to reach and attract the people you need, and then you've got a whole "Selection Process" with different "Selection Criteria" and "Tools", "Policies", "Procedures", varying degrees of involvement from different people in your company. Hell, you need to start the process with some sort of "Position Profile" or whatever label you want to employ, in order to get your recruiting initiative started.

But it boils down to "getting the people I need" in order to get the job done. As a manager you can do it yourself, you can get HR to help you or you can hire a fancy and expensive "Executive Search Firm" which will charge you enough money to make you believe they're adding value ("they must be damn good, we're paying them a fortune!").

Setting targets can be dressed up as "Strategic Planning and Execution", "Organization Development", "Right-Sizing" (or "Down-Sizing", or "Wrong-Sizing", I suppose, when you screw it up),"Delegating", "Managing By Objectives and Results", or more recently "Empowerment", "Performance Standards", "SMART Objectives", "Self-Managing Teams" and other buzz-words. It all boils down to "does everybody know what they're supposed to do?", "does everybody know what is expected of them?".

Training implies that you need to teach somebody how to do what needs to be done. If the people already know how to do it, you can skip it and go to the next step. In a typical modern organization, "Training" is nowadays considered a "bad" word. We prefer to talk about "Learning", and "Career Development", "Coaching and Mentoring", "Talent Management" (a broad term that actually includes the whole 'R-STAR' process focusing on your 'star' people), creating a "Learning Organization", "Change Management" (which is basically teaching people to do things in a different way, or teaching them to do different things).

Appraising involves correcting direction, by providing feedback in order to improve performance. A common mistake made by organizations is to think of appraisal as a way of judging people as "good" or "bad". That is not the purpose of performance appraisal. The purpose of any appraisal scheme is essentially to improve performance. Don't ever forget that. It can be dressed up as "360 degrees feedback", "Performance Appraisal", "Performance Coaching" or any other label you prefer, or it can be as simple as having an informal conversation with each of the people who work in your team about how they're doing their work. The more often you can do it, the better.

Rewarding is about providing consequences. It can be done in financial terms, such as merit increases, bonuses, incentive schemes, profit sharing and the like, and it can be non-financial recognition, such as "employee of the month", "deal of the year" contests, "President's Award", a gold watch when you complete 25 years with the firm, or just being praised (in public or in private). It also involves negative consequences to avoid repetition of undesired behavior, including written warnings, suspensions, admonishments, demotions, transfers to a less rewarding role, or firing. The important thing here, so often overlooked, is that people will do what they're rewarded for, and not necessarily what they're asked to do. IT's amazing how often companies ask people to do one thing (such as cooperate with your colleagues and cross-sell) and yet reward them for something different (such as selling your own products and managing the costs of your own unit). This is the bit that usually screws everything else up, when it is not aligned with the other components of the cycle or does not fit with the "Whole".

Pretty simple and straightforward, huh? Well, it's certainly much easier said then done. Especially when we get into doing it across different cultures.

The culture thing

Managing people is difficult enough (albeit simple) when everybody shares a common culture, that is: everyone shares a common general understanding of what is "right" and what is "wrong", what is "accepted behavior" and what is considered "inappropriate" or "unacceptable". When people in the team have different cultural backgrounds, or the manager's background differs from the team's, that's when things have an enormous potential for serious misunderstandings.

It starts already in **Recruiting**. What is "a good candidate"? In Individualistic societies, people who are outspoken and express strong opinions. In Collectivist societies, people who are relatively modest and who demonstrate they are "well connected". In "Masculine" societies, people who express self-confidence and a "can-do" attitude. In a "Feminine" society, people who are modest, who avoid "standing out" and who ask intelligent questions without appearing too critical. I guess you can quickly see that if whoever is doing the recruiting comes from a different background than the one a candidate is coming from, big mistakes can be made by foregoing excellent candidates who do not match the culturally biased expectations of the recruiter. How do you position yourself as an employer? That is one thing in the US (high on the Masculinity dimension) and a very different thing in The Netherlands and the Scandinavian countries (high on Femininity). How should you do it in

China? That will be mostly influenced by the high Power Distance and the low Individualism, but what does it mean, in practice? You need to understand the impact culture is having on the recruiters, and the impact it has on the candidates you are considering.

Setting targets can be a very different exercise in The Netherlands and in Belgium, two bordering countries which share very little besides a mutual border. Failure to recognize such significant cultural differences between neighboring countries has led to many an acquisition failure, most notably and recently the take-over of ABN AMRO by Fortis, which resulted in the virtual bankruptcy of Fortis and the nationalization of both by the Dutch and Belgian governments. In Feminine cultures like The Netherlands and Scandinavia, targets are negotiated, rather than set by senior managers, and are constantly re-negotiated and adjusted due to "increasing insight". In Masculine societies like the UK, targets are set by management and regarded as a welcome challenge to be overcome by motivated staff. In the UK, negotiating targets is de-motivating. In Scandinavia, targets set by senior managers are perceived to be an abuse of authority (and therefore, de-motivating). So how would you go about setting targets in Switzerland? How do you delegate in India? If you don't adapt to each culture, this quickly becomes a mess.

Let's consider **Training** (and all its derived formulations, as previously mentioned). Learning happens very much centered on the instructor, in societies with a high Power Distance. In societies with low Power Distance, learning experiences should be more interactive and learner-centric, stimulating debates and case studies. In societies with a high Power Distance, pupils tend to participate less in debate, avoid challenging the instructor, and rather depend on the instructor to tell them how to do things. The expectations around Career Development and Talent Management are very different in Anglo-American companies when compared to Latin-American firms. So what happens when an American company tries to implement its global Talent Management program in Guatemala, exactly the same way as it was done in Chicago? It won't happen as smoothly, to say the least... It might actually backfire and cause a lot of people to leave the company, having the exact opposite effect from what was originally intended. This does not mean that you should not have Talent Management programs in Guatemala. It means that they need to be adapted and positioned in a customized way, in order to be effective. Otherwise, they are counter-productive.

Appraisal is another clear example of how the extension of Anglo-American models to different cultures can go completely wrong. Most of the existing management literature is actually written in the US and in the UK, a product of the cultures of these two countries. Providing frank, direct, feedback has been promoted as "the right way" of improving performance anywhere on the planet. It actually works fine in Individualistic, Masculine cultures with low Power Distance, like the UK and US. This notion fails to acknowledge that in Collectivistic, Feminine cultures with high Power Distance (which are present in much more countries on the planet) such procedures are seen as disgraceful and disrespectful. So how do you provide feedback without being perceived as shamefully rude and insensitive? How do you engage people to improve performance? In fact, it is much easier to engage people in most Latin and Asian cultures than in the US or Northern Europe, but the approach needs to be totally different.

Reward, the component that can often screw up everything else, and often does, is totally culture- sensitive. The cash-oriented approach of individual performance-related bonuses hailed in the US and UK as the only way to get people going (pay-for-performance schemes are promoted globally from an Anglo-American perspective), falls on its face when it reaches countries with a more Feminine culture, in which greater responsibility, larger span of control, wider territories, are perceived to be more relevant than cash rewards (which are considered "petty", "mercantilist", "reductionist" and "narrow-minded"). Wouldn´t it be great if we could just solve people motivation issues by throwing money at them, anywhere in the world? If it works for some companies in the US and the UK, why wouldn´t it work everywhere? Well, you need to adapt, again. Bonus plans will work in other cultures, but they need to be tied to other criteria. In some cultures, team incentives work much better than individual rewards. Find out more about the culture you will be operating in, before assuming that what works well in "Place A" has got to work equally well in "Place B".

The global solution

There isn't one. Or rather there are many, different solutions for different cultures, rather than a "one size fits all". You can manage people by applying the "R-STAR" cycle anywhere in the world, but in each culture the cycle needs to be adapted. Different tools are effective in different cultures, for each step in the cycle.

In order to be more effective, start by finding out what are the values of the culture (or cultures) you will be operating in. Where do the people in your team come from? What is their cultural background? Do your homework. Prepare.

I know a manager who turned around a manufacturing plant in Eastern Europe from loss making to profit, simply by applying his scarce knowledge of Hofstede's Five Dimensions of Culture model, putting it into practice. His company thought he was a "miracle maker" and promptly transferred him to Mexico, to deal with another problem-ridden plant. Voilà! New "miracle". The guy again applied his knowledge of the model (different culture, different approach) and suddenly the business was viable. In both cases, his predecessors were good managers, but they only knew how to operate in the environment they were coming from (in this case, France). Our hero simply took the time to read about the culture he was coming into and to adapt his approach in a way that made him readily understood and appreciated by the team he was beginning to lead. Everybody won.

You can do the same in your company, with your team (present and future). In times of stress, such as the crisis we are now facing, many people naturally turn to regression towards the behaviors that worked for them in the past. They "hide under the bed" because that worked for them when they were kids. They repeat whatever got them a promotion five years ago. Don't do that. It would be a stupid thing to do now.

Rather, try to look at the situation you're facing, with fresh eyes. What is the culture background that underlies the operation? What is your own culture background? Do these things match? Do you understand that you have been taught a "right" way to manage which is completely biased by your own culture? There is no "right" way to manage per se, only ways that are effective in some cultures and not effective in others.

Begin by understanding your own culture, your own culture bias. That will make it easier to understand other cultures and other biases, and to bridge the gaps. If we all had a better understanding of each other's cultures and of the impact this has on how business happens around the world, maybe we wouldn't even be in this mess in the first place!

3. Proud To Be Mixed

Is this the beginning of the end? Are we beginning to slowly fulfill the prophecies of Nostradamus about the Apocalypse, moving towards the destruction of the world through a war between East and West? Have we come to the point where cartoons in Scandinavian newspapers have the same detonation power as the terrorist actions of 9/11? Or is everyone overreacting? It's not easy to make sense out of the headlines you see on the media these days. It seems very much that we are moving to increased radicalization of opinions, right and left, and mankind seems to be taking several steps back, rather than progressing towards global understanding and harmony.

In trying to resolve the "East vs. West" conflict, why not look at the South, for a different perspective?

I'm a Brazilian National living and working in Europe for over eleven years. I have watched with concern the increasing debate around globalization, culture clashes all over the world, and more recently the clashes between "the East and the West", notably in different parts of Europe. I've seen it in the media expressed as conflicts between Turks and Germans, Moroccans and French, Arabs and Europeans, Muslims and Christians, etc. It seems that as the European Union started enlarging its membership, a sensitive nerve has been touched. Many people oppose Turkey joining the European Union on the grounds that "the Turks are not European". "They have a different culture from 'ours'".

In the first place, let's remind ourselves that the European Union is not about culture. It is essentially an economic cooperation union, which is something quite different. Many Americans have made the mistake of forecasting the failure of the European Union because "you can never unify such different cultures". Well, guess what? It's not about the unification of culture; it's about economic cooperation!

"Globalization", a term used loosely to name many different things, is similarly not about culture, but rather about economic interdependencies. National and regional cultures will remain differentiated (actually, they tend to become even more differentiated then they are today). Many authors have pointed that out repeatedly, but I'll mention just two: Geert Hofstede and Alvin Toffler, who've been saying this for over 30 years! Will somebody from the press please listen?

There are two different issues at stake here: one is economic cooperation; the other is culture diversity coexistence.

Economic cooperation should continue expanding. Trade barriers should continue to be reduced. Turkey should be allowed to join the European Union, as I believe the economic advantages of that outweigh the economic disadvantages. But there will be many discussions about that, and it will take time (years) before it is settled.

But let's look at the cultural coexistence angle. This is the angle that touches people's emotions, and it sells more newspapers.

I believe globalization will work out, eventually. Fighting against it is futile. Mankind has been evolving towards globalization since the Stone Age, and if we didn't evolve towards it we would still be living in tribes and beating each other up with sticks. It won't mean unifying cultures, but rather learn to coexist respecting each other's increasingly different cultures.

When I look around me today, however, I suddenly realize that we haven't evolved as much as I initially thought: we have larger tribes and bigger sticks, but the stereotyping, discrimination and prejudice is frighteningly similar to what it was more than 1,000 years ago. A picture in the International Herald Tribune, of a policeman on horseback equipped with a helmet and long stick, charging against a mob of protesters in Israel, looked straight out of Ridley Scott's film "Kingdom of Heaven", depicting the Crusades in the Twelfth Century.

I still believe in the benefits of globalization, but we do need to do something about the process and begin deliberately managing the changes, rather than consider ourselves victims of the process and restrict ourselves to defensiveness and resistance. We need to give globalization a different shape and form, or else it might actually not work, after all. Einstein once warned against "underestimating the stupidity of mankind". Indeed, as a species we still have the capacity to be so stupid that we just might end up shooting each other to extinction, so we need to realize the threats and the opportunities involved, and we will need to make some courageous choices to manage change towards a positive outcome.

In the midst of the on-going debates, I've seen comparisons between the different "models" of cultural integration adopted by different countries in integrating (or attempting to integrate) immigrants in their communities. I've read articles on the way the Americans do it (I wouldn't call it integration, but rather "become Anglo-Saxon or remain in a ghetto for generations"), the way the British do it (not very different from the Americans, which is not surprising since the American and British are much more similar than either would like to admit, anthropologically and philosophically speaking), the way the Germans do it (and the debate in Germany now seems to be whether their model of integration should change more towards the Anglo-American "love it or leave it" approach) and the way the French do it (riots in France speak volumes about how successful that approach has been to date).

Please forgive my Brazilian bias (we all have our cultural biases, no exceptions) and allow me to invite you to look at the "Brazilian model". It can hardly be called a model, perhaps, because I don't believe what happened in Brazil throughout the 20th Century was actually planned, but there are lessons to be learned from what happened there, and such lessons might make the difference between global evolution and global destruction.

Brazilian society is far from perfect, actually riddled with deep problems that should not be emulated. I am not advocating Brazilian society as an example, not at all. What I am saying is, let's take a look at the cultural integration of immigrants in Brazilian society, and whether there is something to be learned from that un-planned process.

Cultural integration of immigrants was not marvelous in Brazil. There was also prejudice and discrimination against the "foreigners" who came. But looking back, it was smoother there than in the U.S. or in Europe. And there are fewer conflicts around it today than you find in the so-called "developed countries". So, what happened?

The answer is: sex! (A very "Brazilian" response, I admit, living up to the stereotype of Brazilians as "sex maniacs", expressed in Rio's Carnaval parades). A more "Western European" way of putting it would be: integration happened at the basic cell-level of society, the family. Immigrants started marrying people outside their original "tribes" and forming new "inter-tribal" families, rather than sticking to the ghetto-restrained relationships.

People started breeding across cultural and ethnic backgrounds, and created a more integrated society (from an ethnical point of view). Brazilians today are not the cause of integration; they are the product of integration.

When a Syrian Muslim married a Portuguese Catholic (just an example) in Brazil, before WWII, cultural conflict was brought into the two families in a very concrete way. It was at first painful and disruptive for all parties involved, but eventually they had to cope with it. Initially the new couple was often ostracized by both families, and ended up having to face all kinds of discrimination in society. It was a long process to establish themselves as respectable in the communities they circulated in. This often took years and sometimes generations of strife. But the offspring of the new "inter-tribal" family were raised in a different family environment, no longer "pure" (as in "limited by") the standards of a single tribe, but rather enriched by the combination of both. Often the arrival of a grandchild brought the two original families closer, setting again a different environment for the upraising of such grandchildren. Regardless of their background, grandparents have a tendency to become much more tolerant of what their grandchildren do than they ever were in regards to their own children.

This new generation of grandchildren typically grew up to again engage in "cross-tribal" partnering, marrying partners coming from (for instance) a Japanese background, Brazilian Indian ancestry or African-Brazilian origins. After four or five generations of this, you have a society which is much richer in terms of its diversity and much more open towards further integration than any of the original cultures ever was. Still plagued with multiple issues, certainly not free from discrimination and prejudice, but much closer to being fully integrated than anything you can see in Europe or in the U.S. today.

What could policy-makers learn from this? For one thing, stop trying to "force" immigrants into integration, stop telling them "you need to abandon your roots and embrace the values of your adopted nation!" It's not that simple. Cultural integration is a two-way street. The culture of the "host" country is also affected by the presence of immigrants, and the sooner everyone accepts that fact, the sooner everyone can move towards the development of a "new" culture, a culture that results from the combination of both cultures (or multiple cultures) rather than imposing one on the others. Have faith in the (true) integration process, for the combined culture will be better than the ones who originated it. Such is the natural law of evolution, not only in nature, but in social and political terms as well.

A second thing is to promote the richness of the "new" culture. Diversity is good for you. Develop the capacity of people to perceive the differences among them as a stepping-stone towards understanding the similarities that lie beneath the apparent differences on the surface. The way a mother expresses love for her baby may be different from one culture to another, but that powerful feeling is the same. A culture that can harbor many different ways of expressing love will be much more gratifying to its participants than one which accepts only one way of such expression.

A third thing is to promote cultural integration in the "family cell", the simplest form of social organization. Foster mixed neighborhoods, mixed schools, "sleep-overs", social events that bring people from different communities together (rather than "the English Club", the "American Society" or "the Catholic Charity Group", which all exclude people who are different). Gather people around common values and efforts that transcend cultural background, such as disaster relief projects, environmental awareness programs or sports (but don't encourage ethnic-based competition such as "the Blacks versus the Jews").

Ethnic groups will exist. I'm not advocating declaring "English Clubs" illegal or anything like that. People need to keep in touch with their past, but with their eyes on the future. Such is the nature of human beings. Children need comforting as well as encouragement to grow up and develop. Cultures work in a similar way. There needs to be room for tradition, for feeling safe in regards to your identity based on your past. But just as children need encouragement to grow and develop, cultures also need encouragement to learn and broaden their repertoire, through interaction with different cultures. Cultures need to form ideals and a vision for their future which transcends their past. Policy makers need to put the emphasis on this, rather than on keeping people locked up in history.

So, Policy Makers: encourage people to be proud to be mixed, rather than ashamed of it. Encourage people to be proud to be mixed, rather than to be proud of being "of pure blood". Take a hint or two from the Harry Potter books. Strive to be remembered in the future as the ones who pushed society towards development, rather than as the ones who tried very hard to keep things as they once were.

Be very much aware that cultural integration is a very slow and often painful process. It won't happen over night. It will meet resistance from the many conservative groups that exist in all cultures.

It will require persistence and patience. But it's worth it. The future of our planet, of our grandchildren, depends on changing the way we approach culture, and shaping a new global society that can be fair and just for all, respecting the past, but creating a future that lies beyond the limitations of any past culture by itself.

4. The United States Of Europe Versus The American Union

The so-called "G20" are about to begin another round of negotiation meetings and I read a lot of arguments in the media about "the American approach" and "the European approach" to the global economic downturn. Some journalists prefer to call it a "crisis"; others talk about a "recession". When will they wake up and realize it's already a "depression"? Who will authorize the media to address their reporters, as in: "OK, guys, you can call it a depression now. Go for it and bring me some news items that will help us sell more newspapers!"

Some people need to find a "demon" to blame for everything that is going wrong. Wasn't it great in the good old days (some 3,000 years ago) when people could blame somebody for the bad weather, the poor crop yield, the waning buffalo herd or the subprime mortgage crisis? Crowds would go running to the local tribe Witch Doctor / Sorcerer / Priest / Economics Commentator and ask: why us? Why did this have to happen to us? Why now, just when I was about to splurge on that new fancy lance with the silver-plated grip? And the guy would say something like "We have angered the gods because there is someone in our midst who has offended them!" The Witch Doctor would pick out someone from the tribe, usually someone who had offended him, rather, and point a long curly finger in accusation: "It is Aigh, the red-headed lass! She is a witch! She has offended the gods and they are now punishing us all! Let's get rid of Aigh and all our troubles will be over! The crops will be good again, the buffalo will come back in great numbers and our home equity will be solvent!"

So Aigh was burnt at the stake and things would improve, and people would be thankful for having such a great Witch Doctor, who could always rate who was good and who was bad, even though he was moody. If things did not improve, people would turn again to the Witch Doctor and he would have to come up with someone else to blame, like, maybe, the other tribe who lived across the pond. The last thing the Witch Doctor would say is to throw it back at the people and tell them: "You're asking me why this happened? I'll tell you: the buffalo are gone because you killed too many and scared them away; the crop is bad because you planted too late and didn't care for it properly; the weather is bad because of deforestation and your mortgage has gone sour because you took in more than you can afford to pay, when the market prices were way too high to be reasonable!"

The moody sorcerer knew that if he said something like that, he would be the one burned at the stake, so instead, he said something like: "It's those people across the pond! We live in a global economy and THEY have scared the buffalo away, THEY have cut down all the trees, THEY have outlawed genetically modified corn and THEY have excess savings, which have caused us to overspend! Let's nuke them!"

NOTE: 3,000 years later, I still don't get how excess savings in one part of the world can actually make people overspend in a different part of the world, but that's what the modern Witch Doctors were saying in 2009.

As we approach the April G20 summit, I can't help but think that this "gathering of the tribes" still has a lot of the same dynamics that were in place 3,000 years ago. Many people in the US are still looking for someone to blame, and lately they have taken to put the blame on Europe. Some New York Times columnists have taken to endorse that view, asking whether Europe "is unable to muster a sense of urgency" in order to come up with a huge "stimulus package" such as the one the US is proposing.

The short answer to that question is: "yes, Europe is ABLE to muster a sense of urgency, but no, Europe does not WISH to muster that sense of urgency in this case."

"Why the hell not?" demands the exasperated American. "Because this is not about what is urgent, this is about what is important!" replies the European, beginning to lose patience with the American. Europe has a different notion of what is the problem and how to respond to it.

It's all about the differences in culture, as Geert Hofstede, the Dutch professor, pointed out through numerous research studies that have been carried out repeatedly in different countries over the years. Hofstede was named one of the Top 20 most influential thinkers of our time (number 16, to be exact) by The Wall Street Journal. So that means even investment bankers should pay attention. I said EVEN INVESTMENT BANKERS IN THE BACK ROW TEXTING THEIR BROKERS

SHOULD DROP THEIR BLACKBERRIES NOW AND PAY ATTENTION! Thank you.

Culture is basically the subjective notion of what is considered "right" and "wrong" in a given group of people, whether it is a team, a tribe or a country. We all have a "cultural bias", that is: everything that is akin to what we know as "acceptable" or "right" in our culture, we consider as "good". Everything that is different from that standard we typically consider as "bad". We learn that in childhood, from our parents, teachers, relatives, and neighbors. As Hillary Clinton famously said, "it takes a village".

The truth is, in terms of different cultures, there is no absolute "good" or "bad", there is just "different". If we are able to understand the differences, we will be better able to communicate and to look together for "a third way" of doing something, a way which is not totally "my way" versus "your way", but a way which is acceptable to us both, coming from different cultures.

Hofstede developed a Five-Dimensional Model to describe culture differences, based on research outcomes and factor analysis. For the sake of simplicity and due to space restrictions, let's just look at one of these dimensions, the one that covers the importance placed on performance and the status derived from it (the US scores high on this dimension, on this side of the spectrum) versus the importance placed on caring for others and "quality of life" (Holland and Scandinavia, for instance, score on this opposite side of the spectrum). Many different studies have found the same results; so don't get hung up on Hofstede specifically. After so many independent studies confirming the same results, the findings are accepted as fact.

"Europe", of course, should not be seen as a single culture. All culture studies carried out in the past 40 years have demonstrated there are striking differences among the European countries. In this dimension, for instance, England scores high, like the US, while Holland and Scandinavia score very low. Let's take a look at the differences between the US and The Netherlands, since a few days ago, on the same page of the International Herald Tribune, there were two articles espousing exactly opposing views. One was written by an American, and the other was written by a Dutchman and a German lady (Balkenende and Merkel, to be precise). The American article demanded swift action from Europe, by providing a bigger financial stimulus package. Balkenende and Merkel, instead, were calling for an overhaul of the international regulatory framework for banks. Both articles were talking above each other's heads, because they had different values in mind as their background.

What it means, in practical terms, is that people born and raised in the US learn a set of principles (the "American Way") that are quite different from the set of principles that children in Holland are brought up with (the "Dutch Way"). Neither of them is "right". Neither of them is "better" than the other. They are simply different.

The American Way

In America it's about two opposing forces coming against each other and a resulting force as an outcome. It's about thesis, antithesis and synthesis. "You're either with me or against me". The enemy and us. Two political parties. Winners and losers. The good guys and the bad guys. Black and white.

The American culture values competition, rules that are perceived as fair, and "winning". People who perform well and "win" get a lot of visibility and status, which are perceived as a direct and deserved outcome from "winning". "Big" and "fast" are valued. Making money is considered a visible way of telling the "winners" from the "losers". Winners become idols, heroes. "Standing out" is good. "Showing off" is accepted, as long as it is related to something you have done well, that you have achieved through fair competition, and that you are therefore rightfully entitled to be proud of. Individual achievement is more valued than team achievement; performance is more valued than effort. There is a bias for action, for deciding, for taking individual responsibility and for getting things done. Challenges are welcome.

The culture expresses itself in many ways and one of them is through popular sayings, such as: "time is money"; "the buck stops here" (meaning "I take responsibility for deciding"), "it's the bottom line that counts", "you're either number one or you're last", "the winner takes it all", "if you've got it, flaunt it", "show me the money".

The high value put on performing in a competition means that a lot of importance is put on having fair rules ("equal opportunity", "anyone can make it in America", "the 'American Dream' is possible for anybody"), and on having a clear, measurable way of establishing whom the "winner" is. Therefore, the importance of being "the fastest" (because that is something that can be clearly measured), "the biggest" (easy to measure), "the richest" (money can be added up and counted). Also visible status symbols like big cars, big houses, big boats, are highly valued because you need to have a lot of money to afford it, and if you can afford it, it's because you have out-performed or out-smarted everyone else. If you cheated to win (like Maddoff) then you must be publicly execrated, handcuffed and chained, imprisoned in a penitentiary, for everyone to see what happens to those who break the rules. Heroes are made into idols. Crooks are made into demons. There is not much room for ambiguity, ambivalence or "gray areas". I'm not saying Maddoff should not be punished. I'm merely pointing out that in a different culture his punishment might even be harsher, but it would be less visible and dramatic.

The media has always been full of lists of "the richest individuals", the "Top 500" Companies (measured in financial terms). Lately other "top" lists have become popular, such as "hottest" movie stars, "best cars", but the criteria is always an issue, because it must be perceived as fair. A panel of judges is often used, but they need to be perceived as knowledgeable and/or using fair criteria.

Being quick is good. Fast food is valued (easy to measure "fast"). The quality of food comes after the speed of service. Size of portions is more important (easy to see). Quality of food, taste, becomes more difficult to gauge. Taste is subjective. Some people like ketchup, others don't. So the emphasis is on what is measurable (size, time) rather than what is not.

Cars are big, the bigger the better. Who can "win" an argument about a car's style? That is so subjective! (Therefore, the competition cannot be clearly settled). Size can be measured.

Even "soft" subjects like sex, are turned into measurable competition. A bigger penis, bigger breasts. A big butt is considered ugly on men and on women, but still it's a matter of size (measureable), rather than shape (subjective preference). A film is "erotic" as determined by the amount of exposed flesh. (I remember years ago reading a movie review in Time Magazine in which they could not understand the reason for the international success of "Emmanuelle", a French erotic film that became an all-time office-box benchmark. "There's hardly as much skin exposed as you will find in any second-class porn film!" complained the reviewer, who could not come to terms with the subjectivity of what is "erotic" and what is not. "Do you have to be French, to be erotic?" he went on. The short answer is: "No, but it helps!")

Gender issues are described as "the war between the sexes" (a competition), while the French say "vive la difference!" "Love is a battlefield" and "I will survive" become war anthems for women. Feminist movements focus on "equal opportunity for women", "equal work, equal pay". Focus is on performance, fair rules, which allow women who perform as well as men do, to be rewarded as well as men are.

The "suing mentality" existing in modern America is precisely because people become profoundly indignant if they think that "the rules are not fair", or that someone has "broken the rules" in order to "win". So what do you do? You sue. You complain to the referee, to the judge (of the competition that is life). And you get money as a tangible outcome (rather than a public apology only).

Because "time is money", I want my stuff "now", not later. Doing something is better than doing nothing. "Shoot first, ask questions later". Companies need to report their financial performance every quarter, and when their performance dips, the share prices plummet. "GM must do more and do it faster" was the headline on March 31.

On CNN a trader was interviewed on "short selling" in the stock market, operating in the futures market betting that a stock price will fall. The interviewer was challenging that concept, arguing that the trader was actually hoping that a company would fail, so that he would make money from betting on that failure, and that was "bad". "What about all the people who will lose their jobs?" asked the interviewer. The trader argued that "in the end, it's the bottom line that counts. I mean, if we are not in this to make money, then what's the point?"

To a Dutchman, being in it "only to make money" would be pointless.

The Dutch Way

In Holland it's about many forces coming together and multiple accommodation. Many political parties. Governing coalitions. Expressing your opinion, but being able to live with something a bit different, to accommodate all the different opinions. "We need to find a way to co-exist, all of us". Nobody wins. Everyone has a good side and a bad side. Shades of gray, nothing is pure black or white.

It's all about reaching consensus, as a group, balancing the different individual interests, rather than one individual deciding. People work in order to get a better standard of living, which will allow them to enjoy life better. Work is a means to an end. They perceive Americans as workaholics for whom work is the purpose of life, rather than the means to enjoy life. "That's stupid", say the Dutch, typically and bluntly (as perceived by others).

"Leveling" with others is more important than "winning". There is conflict, like in the States, but the desired outcome is more of a tie, rather than a winner and a loser. People are no pushovers. They can be quite stubborn and obstinate. But the purpose is rather to "stand your own ground" and earn respect, not necessarily to overpower your opponent and stand out from the group as a clear winner, above the remains of your fallen opponent.

There is a lot of sympathy for "the underdog", so people who are clear "winners" feel a bit guilty and sorry for the guy they've just beaten. In politics, often the more aggressive candidate does NOT get the votes, but rather the other guy, who was being more considerate and respectful, and suffering the verbal attacks, is perceived as having the moral quality to be elected. The aggressive one becomes the "bad" guy. By contrast, in the recent US presidential campaign, Obama was often criticized by his own supporters for not being aggressive **enough.**

The Dutch are pragmatic, which is reflected on their attitude towards highly contentious issues like drugs, sex, abortion, euthanasia, immigration. They look at reality and say, "this is happening, it would be foolish to deny it. What can we do, in practice, to improve an existing situation?" So prostitution is legalized as an occupation, and it is taxed as such. People get medical assistance, and STDs are kept under control. "Soft" drugs are tolerated within "coffee-shops", a safer environment. As a result, overall drug use is much less than in nearby France and England. Abortion and euthanasia are commonplace. They don't even make the news anymore. And illegal immigrants get medical assistance, to keep public health at one of the highest levels in the world.

In Holland, you should savor life, in a simple, humble and dignified way, just like everybody else. Everyone is entitled to relaxing and enjoying life, which is more important than performing at work. Therefore, when the clock strikes five, everyone leaves immediately (to go home, to meet friends, to go shopping, to "live"). There are frequent debates about "work and life balance", because "work" and "life" are perceived as two very different entities (this seems very strange to some other cultures, in which "work" is perceived as "part of your life", rather than something different from it). Actually, in practice, people stop working and start preparing to leave 15 minutes before closing time, so that when the clock strikes the hour, shops and offices are already shut and staff are walking to their bicycles. Many times I've found myself in a shop just before closing and the shop staff announce loudly "we're closing now!" People (tourists, the locals are used to it) look around surprised. A lady asks "but it's ten to six, don't you close at six?" The reply is "Yes, but we have a life too, you know! It's time for us to go!" I guess the concept of "the client is always right" never made it to Dutch retail.

Showing off is frowned upon. It is perceived as arrogance, and deeply disapproved of. Typical sayings are "Be normal, that's crazy enough" and "If you stick your head up, it will be chopped off".

Gender issues are about getting men to be more "feminine" (sensitive, helping to care for children, caring for the home) as much as they are about opportunities for women to play traditionally "masculine" roles. Many women choose to work fewer days a week, or choose not to pursue a corporate career towards top management. "Who wants to be a workaholic?" they say. "I can live a full life doing other types of satisfying work, as a professional or running my own business. I don't want to spend my life in a corporate office!" Work-at-home dads are more common than in the US.

Being quick and fast is considered a sign of being superficial and shallow. Long-term relationships are more important than short-term results. Holland recently celebrated 400 years of uninterrupted commerce with Japan, the only Western country to do so. Companies are not evaluated by quarterly results, but rather by their long-term potential and their history of stability.

Regular business meetings happen every two weeks, rather than weekly. When people ask "can I have it immediately", the answer is "yes, of course, in two weeks". Life has its rhythm (apparently, a two-week rhythm), which must be respected.

When Americans say "we need a big stimulus plan, and we need it now", the Dutch say, "Wait a minute! Rushing into something is stupid! Rushing into things and overspending is what got everybody in trouble in the first place. Let's look at the situation carefully and discuss it with all stakeholders involved, aiming for consensus. If you try to do something quick and dirty, you will regret it later. Let's make sure we do it right, so we don't have to do it two or three times!"

The Americans think, "These Dutch guys are impossible! They're not DOING anything and time is running out!"

The Dutch think, "these Americans are not human beings, they're 'human doings!' They want to run off, jump on a horse and ride madly off in five different directions! They need to aim before they fire, rather than 'shooting from the hip'!"

In Holland, "to be" is more important than "to have". In the US, people ask, "what do you mean, 'to be'? What is that supposed to mean?"

I have a Brazilian friend who was an expat in the US and, a few years later, was an expat in Holland. He told me that when he arrived in America, the first thing he did was he bought a red Ford Mustang. To him it was a symbol of "being successful in America". When he moved to Amsterdam, years later, I met him there. "So, what kind of car did you get in Amsterdam? A Mustang is probably too big for the narrow streets..." I asked. He said, "I've been here for eight months and I still didn't get a car, maybe I will never get one. I have my bicycle and I ride the trains. None of my colleagues have cars. It's a very different lifestyle."

The G20 meeting

Americans want more money for stimulus, and they want it now. The Dutch want to wait a bit to see the effect on the economy of the money that has already been committed in the first stimulus packages. They think that you need to allow some time for the impact to be felt. It's a bit like drinking beer: It takes some time to feel slightly "high". If you drink too much and too quickly, as soon as you feel "high" you will also feel "drunk" and totally sick. You stop drinking, but it's already too late. You throw up and you pass out. A nice night out with your friends ends in a hospital enjoying a stomach pump. So what's the point? Drink slower and enjoy it. Stop increasing your liquidity before you feel sick.

The Dutch fear that too much money in circulation will create inflation, a bigger problem than a recession, because it creates concentration of income, "winners" and "losers", when "leveling" is more important to them. They feel that changing banking regulatory frameworks is more important, to avoid another crisis, and it will take time to implement, so it's better to start working on it now, to avoid problems in 2011. More money now is not a solution, it creates a bigger problem.

Americans say that Europe is adrift; there is no clear direction. Europeans see themselves as "steady on course" for the long run. They see America zigzagging right, left and center, changing direction every month.

The approaches are not "right" or "wrong". They are simply "different". They stem from different mindsets.

The thing is, you cannot convince a Dutchman with "American" arguments, just as you cannot persuade an American with "Dutch" arguments. You need to find a "third way" to reconcile the conflict. Perhaps the Indians or the Brazilians will offer some suggestions. But people will need to understand their own cultural biases, and each other's biases, before they can open their minds to a "third way".

5. Are We On A Boat Or Part Of A Shopping Mall?

Kishore Mahbubani, dean of the Lee Kuan Yew School of Public Policy, National University of Singapore, has written an article on the IHT titled "A rudderless world" (19 Aug 2011). He describes the world as "...people living in more than 190 cabins on the same boat. Each cabin has a government to manage its affairs. And the boat as a whole moves along without a captain or a crew."

According to Mr. Mahbubani, "the demand for global leadership has never been greater. The world is truly lost in trying to find a way out of the current crisis." I would like to provide a different perspective.

Who needs a leader?

The need for leadership is culturally determined. Different cultures express different needs for different kinds of leaders. Research shows that in Singapore hierarchy and respect for authority are much more highly valued than, for instance, in Northern Europe and North America. For every Singaporean who wants strong leadership to "run the boat", there is an American Tea Party member who wants less leadership, and more autonomy and freedom for all those different people living in the 190 different cabins. The "need for leadership" needs to be qualified.

Margaret Thatcher once said, "There is no such thing as 'society'. Everyone should look after themselves." A fine example of individualist, "low power distance" thinking, which is predominant in North America and Northern Europe. Research also shows that, on the other hand, most of the world's population live in "hierarchical" societies. Outside of Northern Europe and North America, practically everybody else is in a "hierarchical" culture, totaling 91% of the world's population. Only 9% of the world's population live in "egalitarian" societies, which include Australia, New Zealand and Costa Rica, in addition to the aforementioned North America and Northern Europe.

If we lived in a planetary democracy, indeed we would choose, as a planet, for a strong leader as Mr. Mahbubani seems to be asking for. However, the reality is that those 9% of "egalitarians" in the Northwestern corner of the world account for 36% of the world's GDP. Their share of production is proportionately much higher than the rest, and that gives them more political clout.

The US alone spends more on its military budget than all the other nations combined. This also tilts the scales towards the Northwest. Still, what has changed in the past 20 years is that connectivity has grown exponentially, and the share of GDP held by "the Northwest" has actually decreased (it was much more in 1970) as emerging markets have developed at a quicker pace (notably China and India, but others as well). Moving forward, the trend is that the economic imbalance between "the Northwest" and "the Rest" will decrease, although it is not likely to disappear entirely.

Mr. Mahbubani points out that "geo-economics require consensus", but "geopolitics of the world are running at cross purposes with the geo-economics of the world." He concludes that "The world is adrift". This is where I think we need to look at this from a different angle. The need for leadership is different, depending on whether you come from Asia or from North America. And if geo-economics require consensus, maybe that means we need a different analogy to guide our thinking.

Ship or Shopping?

The metaphor of being on a ship and needing a captain to tell the crew how to run the ship and how to "look after" the passengers in the cabins is a very hierarchical one. It assumes that all parties involved share "hierarchical" values, which is not the case. It also plays down the notion of sovereign states. Granted, this notion is outdated and will be replaced by a different political order. However, this will be a long process, lasting perhaps yet another 20 or 30 years, if not more.

Our situation at present is more akin to that of 190 shop owners in a shopping mall. We form a kind of condominium that needs to be managed, but the mall manager does not hold the same kind of authority as the captain of a ship. The shop owners may appoint someone for the role of mall manager, but they have complete authority in managing each their own shop. From time to time, they need to meet in a sort of assembly, to decide on certain broad issues, such as opening hours, shared services such as security, cleaning, waste management, energy consumption. The analogy to Planet Earth is clearer than thinking of a ship.

The mall manager of Planet Earth needs to be more of a coordinator, rather than a captain. Mr.Mahbubani argues that Barak Obama is "the best candidate for global leader". I agree, but only if he relinquishes the presidency of the US (to Sarah Palin? Rick Perry? Hillary Clinton?). The mall manager cannot manage the mall and simultaneously manage the largest shop in the mall.

One might argue that the mall manager is the Secretary General of the United Nations. I would say that the UN has become too bureaucratic and has lost much of its legitimacy. It needs to be replaced by another institution, with a similar purpose but a different mandate. We need a fresh institution with a different governance model, perhaps with an Economic Council made of the G20 and a different arrangement for the Security Council.

The irony in the US is that Obama may not get re-elected, because people in the US want a leader that is aggressive, decisive and bold. They want a cowboy type like a Texan, but with the intellect of a Bostonian. Those two archetypes seldom come together... and having to choose between the two, Americans may go for the stupid cowboy rather than the wimpy intellectual. Yet, if there were global elections to appoint a global leader, Obama would win by a landslide.

The Crisis Of Democracy

Mr. Mahbubani asks: "Have democracies become dysfunctional?" I would say the short answer is: "Yes. But only temporarily and only in very specific parts of the world." Anglo-Saxon democracies, notably the US and the UK, have become dysfunctional. For how long, we don't know. The US is paralyzed due to their "Competition" model of governance pitting Democrats against Republicans. They need a "third force" to solve the impasse. The UK is in crisis because of their similar model, pitting Labor against Conservatives. None managed to secure a majority in the last election, so they had to form a coalition, which has found it difficult to manage the economic issues.

However, one should not judge Europe by looking at the UK. And we should never judge Europe looking at it through the eyes of the UK, either. The European Union is all about trying to reach consensus through coordination. This profoundly irritates advocates of the Anglo-Saxon model of decisive leadership, and it also annoys very much all those living in hierarchical societies, who expect a strong, authoritarian leader, even if they might not like the person currently in that position and would prefer someone else. However, the EU is not hierarchical and it is not Anglo-Saxon. It has a diversity of values and of governance models which demands something different from the simple “top-down” approach found in hierarchical societies and also different from the decisive model valued in the US and UK.

Northwestern democracies need renewal, yes. The bad news for the Anglo-Saxon advocates and for the hierarchical advocates is: in a multilateral world with a more balanced distribution of power among the US, Europe, China and a couple of other key players, the more appropriate leadership style may be the coordinator, the” mall manager”, rather than the ship captain.

The Dutch and Scandinavian cultures have had such governance models running for at least a few hundred years, maybe more. They have some of the best Human Development scores in the world, so they must be doing something right... We need to look at that more closely, for therein may lay the best alternatives for the world going forward.

6. Bankers and Bankers

I've worked as a Human Resources executive in three different banks for a total of 28 years over the past 35 years of my professional life. The other seven years I've spent in consulting, most of the time for non-banking organizations. As a bank employee, I always took pride in identifying myself with the business I was in, rather than with my functional expertise. I introduced myself, filled in forms, and responded to questions as "a banker", rather than as "an HR professional". I believed (and still do) that the best way that all "staff" functions (such as HR, Finance, IT, Legal, Admin) can add value to their organizations is by fully identifying and understanding the business purpose of their organizations. I took courses on banking, on financial products and markets, I took part in discussions about risk management, distribution channels, pricing and cash flow management with my colleagues in these bank's management teams.

I thought of banking as a gatherer of scarce (financial) resources in the economy, which then redistributed these resources in the form of loans to the most effective project proposals (private and corporate). In return for gathering money, analyzing the validity, risk, and potential return of different proposals, and deciding on loans to finance such proposals, banks were allowed to charge a fee for their services, in the form of interest. In other words, the social purpose of banks is to add value to the economy through risk management. When they do their job well, people will pay enough interest to cover the costs of a bank's staff and infrastructure, plus provide enough profit to allow for a proper return on investment to its shareholders and leave enough money to re-invest in growing the efficient business of that bank.

Performing this role well means that a bank has more impact on society than any other industry, because it actually touches every industry in the economy, including other banks. We were able to recruit a lot of young talented people because they wanted to "change the world". What better way to do that, than to join a company that had such big impact on all other companies and on all individuals as well?

If a bank does not perform well, it will loan money to the wrong projects, will not make enough revenue to cover its costs, and will go bankrupt. If a bank performs well, but charges too much money in fees for its services and is perceived as "ripping off" its customers (private and corporate), it will eventually incur in the wrath of clients and regulators, and lose its "license to operate", either from the action of regulators, or from seeing its clients take their business elsewhere.

For several years this picture was clear in my mind and I often used it as a reference whenever I was involved in recruiting talented people for the organizations I worked for, especially for ABN AMRO in Amsterdam and Banco Real in Sao Paulo.

One day I was talking to my two youngest daughters, who were in primary school in those days, and they asked me: "Daddy, what do you do in your work?" I told them: "Daddy is a banker!"

They stared at me with wide eyes. One of them asked, "what is a banker?" to which the other responded before I could say anything: "You know, those big guys with a big hat and a coat which throw the little girl out of her house!" I was stunned.

The youngest countered: "Nah, but Daddy's not a bad guy... Right Daddy?" The other looked at me again, waiting for my reaction. My response was: "Well, there are good bankers and bad bankers. The guy you saw on TV was a bad banker, who throws people out of their homes if they don't pay back the money they borrowed from him. But I don't do that; in my bank we don't do that. We lend money to people to make their dreams come true, like when they want to buy a new house, or a car, and they don't have the money, we lend them the money and they can use it to buy what they want, and they can give me my money back later, a little bit at a time, when they get money from their work".

This was already a long enough explanation for them, so they changed the subject and moved to something else. They were satisfied. I was not.

I kept thinking about it for several days. I discussed it with colleagues at work. I made a big issue about it.

This was the image my kids had about bankers. It was probably the image most people had: bankers are bad guys in dark suits, exploiting little girls and their grannies. They are greedy, heartless SOB's, who derive satisfaction from driving people to the poorhouse. What happened to the story about redistributing scarce resources to develop the economy? It didn't get told very often. Not many people heard it at all, and of those who did, probably very few really believed in it.

As I discussed it with my fellow bankers, I found that many of them did not care. I soon realized that there were, indeed, "good" bankers and "bad" bankers, or perhaps "soft" bankers and "hard" bankers, according to their style of behavior.

The soft bankers were those few who did care, and who believed their work was helping make this a better world. They were also concerned about the image that bankers had and they believed that the success of their business was actually based on trust, something rather "soft" and "fuzzy" that was difficult for a banker to cope with specially if you were brought up with hard figures and financial math as the needed skills for what you did.

The "hard" bankers had a very different mindset. They basically felt that life is a competition, and whoever makes the most money wins. These were bankers, who accepted the negative image of banking as a fact of life, something that they could do nothing about, and something that was in the mind of ignorant people who did not understand what life is really about. Why worry about what others think, especially if they are ignorant and not capable of making a lot of money in their own businesses?

The "hard" bankers had little concern about the "meaning" of what they did; it was all about doing a good job by making a lot of money, for the company and for themselves. They based their success on technical expertise and rational thinking. The "soft" bankers were concerned about the meaning of what they did; it was all about helping other people and businesses (though certainly not by giving away money for free). They based their success on relationship skills and building trust.

As I explored the issue further, trying to better understand the mindsets of "hard" bankers and "soft" bankers, I came across another division. Most of the "soft" bankers were in consumer banking (with honorable exceptions) and most of the "hard" bankers were in Investment Banking and Capital Markets (again with notable exceptions to confirm the rule).

...And Then Investment Banking Was Created

Bankers in general are a conservative lot. They are risk-averse. They are not innovative. In 1978 I was at an international conference on Organization Renewal, debating with Organization Development specialists who worked in different industries and different countries. When I described enthusiastically the innovative programs I was starting to run in my own company, they were all very interested. When I told them I worked in a bank, they practically laughed me out of the room. "You're out of your mind", they said. "Those things will never work in a bank! Banks are too conservative. They are huge bureaucratic, crystallized structures averse to change and innovation. The new frontiers of management are in chemicals, oil, consumer goods, the auto industry, not in banks."

A few years later, Anthony Hourlihan, a consultant in Financial Services, addressed an audience of 200 young talents from an international bank: "I will not lie to you. Banking is boring. If you go to a bar tonight and you meet a beautiful girl, and when you tell her that you are in banking she smiles and says 'how exciting!' let me give you some advice: do not marry that girl! She is lying to you. Banking is not exciting, it's boring. People may be attracted to the fact that you can make a lot of money in this business, but I can mention 50 other things that are more exciting then banking".

If banking was so boring, how did banks create new products and services? They followed their clients. When clients starting doing international business, banks became international. When clients invented sophisticated cash management systems for their companies, banks copied those and offered them to all companies. Credit cards, ATMs, international money transfers, project finance, all products and services that we take for granted as "banking products" were actually created outside of banks and later adopted by banks when their clients demanded it. I've even seen companies who developed software, in-house, and came to their bank saying: "here, if you use this software which I am giving you for free, you can process our invoice collection much faster than you currently do, and turn out reports in a format that is much more user-friendly and useful for us. You will probably find it attractive for other clients as well." I've been a witness to this.

In the late seventies and early eighties, companies started getting creative about finding sources of capital. They invented new ways of raising capital and passed it on to the banks. Why was it so? Banks were big fat cats, conservative and contented. There was no need for innovation. They were used to clients coming up to them and asking for finance, and they would just say "no" if they were not comfortable with the risk, or if they simply did not have enough capital available.

Necessity is the mother of invention. The necessity was on the companies' side. Entrepreneurs needed capital, so they started inventing new ways of raising it, new creative formulas of enabling banks to lend more money. Entrepreneurs still needed the banks as vehicles. Only banks had the asset gathering capabilities and the distribution channels required by new ways of underwriting capital, organizing IPOs, syndicated loans, and securitization.

Banks also were the only organizations with the legal license to carry out some of these activities. Some entrepreneurs attempted to do some of this outside the banking industry, but they were sued out of the market, crashed down by regulators or boycotted by banks in such a way that none of them became significant players. A few banks were bolder than others, and started adopting some of this new-fangled stuff. This forced the others to adopt the new practices too, or risk losing clients to competitors. Many times I witnessed internal discussions in banks in which a proponent of a "new" product argued with risk managers and legal experts who advised against it: "But all our competitors are doing this! If we don't do it too, we'll be out of the market!"

In the US there was Glass-Steagall, a law separating "investment banking" from "commercial banking" activities, to avoid conflicts of interest and keep risk at bay, but in other parts of the world there was no such separation. American bankers lobbied intensely for years and finally got the law revoked.

Investment banking, as an economic activity, grew tremendously. The products that had been created outside of banks were creating a windfall for banks and firms involved in it. People started getting paid handsomely for the deals they made. Young talent flowed to "Wall Street" and to banks all over the world, and away from engineering, manufacturing and the caring professions.

The Human Side of Banking (not kidding)

Banking, suddenly, became attractive. Hollywood films started to show a new image of bankers: glamorous, smart, sexy. "Working Girl", "91/2 Weeks" showed sexy, smart, young people doing all kinds of clever things. And they were bankers! Even "Wall Street", in which the main character is the "bad guy", who did they cast in that role?

Michael Douglas, at the height of fame and glamour. "American Psycho" was a horror film about a serial killer, but it was also a panorama of investment banking and it cast young Christian Bale as the axe-wielding heartbreaker.

In the nineties, young talented people wanted to be in banking. And they didn't mean consumer banking. They all wanted corporate finance. There were 10, 20 candidates for each vacancy. The more difficult it became to get into, the more attractive it became for young men and women who loved challenge. Soon there were 50 candidates to a single job. Only the best would get it.

And exactly who were "the best"? I can tell you: they were the "hard" bankers. The people selected were the ones who had the "hard" skills: strong in math, creative, quick, flexible, "driven" (as in willing to work long hours on special deals), persistent. Nobody was looking at "ethics" as criteria in those days. Relationship skills? Yes, that was "desirable", but not a requisite. Engineers started dropping out of their jobs in mechanics, electronics, production and chemistry, and started moving to structured finance, treasury and capital markets.

Within banking organizations, "culture wars" began to emerge. Investment bankers looked down on commercial bankers. They saw commercial bankers as "old fashioned", "back-slappers" who did not have the brains to make it in the "brave new world" of modern banking. Commercial bankers were "good at making friends, that's all. Anybody can do that. They couldn't understand how to manage a 'yield curve', they couldn't recognize derivatives if they bit them on their assets."

Commercial bankers, in turn, despised the young newcomers to the industry. They saw investment bankers as "back-stabbers" who "would do anything for a deal, opportunistic SOBs who did not value long-term partnerships with clients. It takes experience to build trust and to be able to 'smell' risk, it takes artful skills and a network in the market to be able to assess who are the clients you can trust, who are the ones you need to avoid. These young kids think life is about 'day-trading' and mathematical models, they have no sense of history nor long-term perspective, they don't realize that banking is all about trust!"

Most banks started to drift towards one end of the spectrum or the other. You either became very good at investment banking or you became very good at consumer and commercial banking. A few organizations tried to become "universal banks", notably Citibank, HSBC and ABN AMRO, as pointed out by The Financial Times in a landmark article in 1997. However, within these three organizations (and elsewhere as well), the culture wars raged on.

The investment banking professionals wanted to emulate Goldman Sachs, Merrill Lynch and Salomon Brothers (in those days). The consumer and commercial banking professionals had Bank of America, Deutsche Bank and Wells Fargo as models. These internal wars consumed a lot of energy, which was diverted from providing better products and services to clients.

The Moral

In his award-winning book "Purpose", Nikos Mourkogiannis outlined that all companies have a moral purpose, even though most often than not they are unaware of it. It is part of their corporate culture, though not always explicit.

Typically, a company's moral purpose falls into one of four categories: Heroism, Altruism, Excellence and Discovery. Companies whose moral purpose falls under "Heroism" are those who focus on beating the competition, being better than anybody else, being "the last one standing" in a fight. Goldman Sachs is one of the examples mentioned by the author. I can say that "heroism" is not the moral purpose only of Goldman, but of most investment banks. The competition is fierce. The products offered are basically the same. In order to succeed, you need to be quicker, smarter, better than your competitor in offering and delivering the same things.

Commercial banking, though, falls under the category of "Altruism". The focus is on the clients, rather than on competitors. Success is based on developing trusting relationships in which the clients believe that the bank is helping them to manage their daily finances, invest for the future and purchase what they want (buy now, pay later).

No wonder there were culture wars going on! When people have different moral purposes it becomes more difficult to work together. Sharing a common goal is a pre-requisite for any team, any company to be effective. These culture wars eventually brought ABN AMRO down from the international arena, and they have many times brought Citi to the brink of bankruptcy (they've shown an amazing capacity to bounce back from every crisis, but only to fall in another canyon shortly after recovering). HSBC has been less damaged by these wars and by the economic crisis, but it has often been "accused" of not being able to develop a strong investment banking business.

The crisis

What happened to cause the mortgage crisis in the US, and the bursting of the derivatives bubble all over the world? Well, it was more of an investment banking problem, rather than a consumer and commercial banking problem. And it was definitely caused by "hard" bankers rather than "soft" bankers.

The bubble started with "over-leveraging", the use of derivatives and securitization to create "artificial capital". Commercial bankers were lending all the money they had. Investment bankers came up with creative ways of allowing banks to lend much more than they had, and of selling the risk of the loans in a secondary market. This secondary market grew out of control and became a kind of "Ponzi scheme". Banks were trading securities among themselves and selling them to institutions all over the world. People lost the link from the securities they were buying back to the mortgage that Mr. Jones was paying in Los Perdidos, California. The whole thing escalated so much, that it became depersonalized. It was all based on statistical models that very few people understood. (A consultant once praised Royal Bank of Scotland, who grew exponentially, because "they have a fantastic set of mathematical Risk Management formulas, which allow them to be better than anybody else at this!") The result: small municipalities in Europe lost millions because they invested in securities issued by banks from Iceland, which had invested in securities issued by Lehman Brothers in New York, who had bought the risk of mortgages issued by… somebody down the line who actually lent the money to Mr. Jones and quickly sold the loan to somebody else. As it turned out, Mr. Jones is still paying his mortgage on time, to this day. But when some of the intermediaries down this daisy chain went bust because they could not pay the loans they had made in order to buy more mortgages, everybody down the daisy chain lost money. The chain was broken in the middle, not in the starting end, with Mr. Jones. He still doesn't know what the whole mess is about.

The first myth that should be dispelled is that it was "surprising", "unannounced" or "inevitable". It was none of these. As early as 2003, I attended senior management meetings in which one of the topics was "the US housing bubble" and when it was due to burst. The discussion was when should we get out of that business, not "if". It was the proverbial party that Warren Buffet often talked about. The party is going great. Everybody knows that it's going to end badly, but nobody wants to be the first to leave and miss out on the fun that is still going on. Yet everybody knows that the last ones to leave are going to have to pay the bill. And, hell, they might even go to jail if they don't have the means to pay the bill!

In the case of those management meetings, the decision was to stay in the mortgage business a bit longer, because the bank was making a lot of money on it. Shareholders were happy, staff got big bonuses, customers bought houses, it was so much fun for everybody. The people saying, "this is going to go bust" were not able to persuade the others to leave the party.

A few years later, the people who wanted to leave finally persuaded the others. The business was sold to Citibank, a real "party animal" with a reputation for buying up everything that others did not want. Citibank lost billions in the mortgage crisis. Other banks avoided losses by selling the business before it went sour.

As the mortgage bubble burst, it triggered a bigger crisis in the credit markets. The problem was not lending money to companies and individuals; it was lending money to other banks. Banks rely on lending to each other to keep the flow of capital eventually reaching businesses and individuals. Suddenly it became very risky to lend money to certain banks, which could go under without paying what they owed, and trigger a domino effect across the banking system, bringing down many banks. The fear of a crisis actually brought on the crisis. When the credit markets froze in midair, Bear Sterns came down, then Lehman Brothers. The domino effect began and it was panic at the disco, I mean, on Wall Street.

This was no surprise. In the seventies I witnessed a crisis affecting banks of a certain region. It was triggered by predatory competition, a pricing war that made several banks start losing money in their efforts to attract customers away from each other's portfolio. There was a high-level meeting of competitors. All the "hard" bankers were there. They made a "gentlemen's agreement" to stop the pricing war.

A week later the war was still raging. A friend of mine, a lawyer, said, "this gentlemen's agreement is fully nullified by absence of the object". I asked him to translate this into English, and he said: "there can be no gentlemen's agreement when there are no gentlemen present!" It did not come as a surprise that, a few years later, that bank went bust. It was nationalized and eventually privatized a decade later.

In the eighties, I witnessed another curious situation. A meeting with the Money Markets team (all of them "hard" bankers) in which the CEO of a bank bluntly said that there was a "bomb" flying around in the market (he actually used porn language which I won't repeat; this is an "R" rated article). He said that all banks were holding their assets against the wall and passing the bomb around, making some money in fees as they did so. Everyone new that the bomb was going to explode on somebody's assets, but no one could predict who would go bust, so he urged the traders to continue playing the game but to be extra careful. Three weeks later, that bomb "exploded". Three banks went down, and that bank was one of them.

So it's no wonder that, when the mortgage bubble burst, we saw similar behavior. Instead of coming together and try to avoid a crisis, it was "every bank for himself": bankers knew that "somebody's going to go down, but it's not going to be me". Actually, they were probably thinking "The less competitors in the market, the better! If many banks go bust, the survivors will get the spoils! We just need to ensure we don't go down with the others, and we'll come out at the top when this is over!" As the Fed and the American Treasury tried to organize a way out, bankers paid no heed. The first banks went under. The Fed started pouring tons of money into the system, but banks kept to their traditional ways: they stood with their assets against the wall and refused to lend to each other. "Somebody else is going to go bust, but it's still not going to be me!"

Since then (mid 2008) the situation has improved, but there's still a bomb flying around, only smaller. Some banks have taken the decision to accept government funds and cede participation on their boards to government officials (in many parts of the world). Some were forced to do it, they had no choice. Others chose to do it following an old saying. "When you see a lot of 'bombs' flying around in a room, be quick: take one of the smaller ones and stick it in your assets. Because you don't want to end up getting stuffed with the bigger bombs!"

By the way, similar principles apply to the Madoff scheme: many people knew about it and got out in time, before the party went sour. And now some banks are making deals with their clients to avoid getting hit by a bigger bomb later.

Lessons

Right now, the "soft" bankers are smiling. The old risk managers, who insisted that knowing their clients was more important than relying on mathematical models are actually laughing out loud. The only reason that they are not laughing even harder is that the crisis eventually hit just about everybody, including them. There's not much comfort in saying "I told you so" when your own house has also been engulfed by the fire which started across the street.

The first lesson is to listen to experience. Don't discount what the old guys have to say. The Spanish say that "the Devil knows more from being old than from being the Devil". I always have to chuckle when I read about "analysts' estimates" about a company's performance or the prospects for the economy. The vast majority of "analysts" in financial institutions are kids with less than five years experience. They have their mathematical methods of analysis, but they haven't yet developed that capability of "feeling" or "smelling" what's going on. That will only come in time, if it comes at all.

The second lesson is to develop your "soft" skills, as well as your "hard" skills. The relationships you form are part of who you are and what you are capable of. In the eighties John Gage, from Sun Microsystems, said that "the network (of PCs) is the computer", as opposed to mainframe computers. In the 21st Century, "the network is the manager". A manager (in any business) without a network of relationships is only half a manager. Also, things like intuition are crucial for being effective, and not only rational thinking. The ability to inspire trust and to assess who to trust and who to be weary of, are not rational skills.

The third lesson is that ethics matters. It comes first. The lack of ethics moved investment bankers from "creative destruction" to "destructive creation". The first concept refers to destroying old practices in order to create newer and better practices. The newer practices are only "better" if they respect ethics. The second concept refers to creating financial instruments (such as derivatives), which eventually blow up in your face.

The last but not least important lesson is that you should always try to expand your horizons in terms of time (think about long-term consequences) and systemic impact (think about how what you do affects others in society, on a global scale). This applies to everything, from the banking system to the environment (think global warming).

Education and learning can hopefully get us out of all the messes we've put ourselves into, but it begins with recognizing that we all have a lot to learn, always. "Masters of the Universe?" They should have known better.

7. Bogus Bonus Brawl

I've been amused, if not amazed, by the public uproar in the US about the 160 million dollars paid as bonus to AIG executives for the year 2008, when the company nearly went bankrupt. There's been a lot of emotion and very little reasoning involved in examining the situation, so let's take a few steps back and try to look at it objectively. This could prove to be more helpful in trying to understand what is going on. Of course, if you're not interested in understanding what is going on, but rather you're one of the many who are just enjoying the fact that there is somebody out there (AIG) that you can blame for everything that is going wrong in the economy, then please stop reading this text and just go out and join the crowds throwing tomatoes at AIG. While you're at it, you can throw a couple of tomatoes on my behalf, but not because of the 160 million in bonuses; rather, throw them because they were so terrible in managing their organization, and because they succumbed to the attraction of a bonus distortion, already years ago.

You may think that a bonus is a bonus is a bonus. Actually, they're not. There are bonuses and bonuses.

A long time ago, in the 20th Century, bonuses were created as a special award for people who had done something extraordinary during the past fiscal year. If the company's performance was especially good, it seemed only fair to take a small portion of the company's profits and pay out a special "prize" to those individuals who had done something outstanding to contribute significantly to that especially good company profit.

After a while, since company profits continued to improve over the years, there was a gradual increase in the number of people who got a bonus award. At first they were "a chosen few"; gradually there were more and more people included in that select group, and soon the group was no longer "select", it was practically everybody, or at least everybody belonging to a certain level in the job structure, or being part of a certain business function.

The practice began to spread to all kinds of industries. The most aggressive bonuses were paid by the investment banks, and in the 1980's they began to make headlines in The Wall Street Journal. I was there. I was an HR director of an investment bank from 1982 to 1989. I designed bonus schemes. I benchmarked our bonus schemes with those of the most successful firms on Wall Street. I hired compensation consultants to provide information on what our competitors were doing, and to help us design bonus plans that were smarter, more attractive to help us recruit talent, more cost-efficient and closely related to performance.

In the late 80's the distortions began to appear in the market. Investment bankers, especially traders and brokers, are basically deal-makers. The best traders are great at making deals and terrible as managers. The best traders started striking deals with their managers that allowed them to negotiate pre-arranged bonuses according to mathematical formulas. There was no longer "management discretion" in setting the value of a bonus; it was all pre-calculated as a percentage of generated profit, or a fixed amount linked to achieving a pre-set target. To me, that is not a bonus. That is a sales commission. That's Distortion Number One.

Then the negotiations started happening at the beginning of each year, linked to target setting. Traders became experts at negotiating small targets, always arguing that the market would be more difficult in the coming year, and walked away with huge bonuses paid for doing what they were supposed to be doing in the first place (making deals). In 1985, the Global HR Head of a leading Wall Street firm told me that, in order to avoid further distortions, compensation at his company used a "three thirds" frame of reference. One third of a trader's annual compensation should come from that person's fixed salary (which should allow the person to live comfortably, and have a nice vacation once a year not far from the job location). A second third of a trader's compensation should come from a performance-based cash bonus scheme. This would allow a good performer to double his/her income, and have a holiday in Europe, or buy a fancy car. The third third should be in the form of long-term incentives or deferred compensation (such as stock options). The idea was that this portion would be designed in such a way that the trader would remain in the company for a few years, rather than jump to the first competitor pirate ship who offered 10% more in fixed or variable pay.

Distortion Number Two is that this rule of thumb, which was already quite aggressive since it allowed someone to double and even triple their fixed income through bonus schemes and long-term incentives, was soon left beside the road. Traders negotiated smaller fixed salaries in exchange for higher bonuses. The reasoning that soon out-smarted their incompetent managers was that, with a small salary, the company risk of hiring an incompetent trader was diminished. A trader would have to be really good to earn enough bonuses just to make a living. If a bad trader was hired by mistake, that person would be punished by having to live off a ridiculously low salary. In order to earn a living, traders had to make a lot of good deals. It became the Wall Street equivalent of the door-to-door salesman, hired with no salary and a high sales commission. In the 90's, bonuses no longer represented 100% of fixed salary, but rather 400% or even 1,000%. And this was thought to be a good thing!...

What people were late to realize was that a trader who depends exclusively on bonus to earn a living will soon start taking more and more risk, just to make ends meet. They also started refusing to do anything that was not directly linked to their bonus scheme. So when a global crackdown on money laundering was initiated by regulators in the early 90's, traders were asking "how will this improve my bonus?" If there was no link to bonus, it was not practiced. Some firms started linking bonuses to ethics and being honest (!!), so that if you were ethical you got a bonus and if you were not, your bonus was reduced by a certain factor (but it was still there).

Bonuses were paid for reaching targets, for being honest, for doing what you were supposed to do in the first place. So, naturally, even companies that were losing money often paid out bonuses to their star traders. The reasoning was that if they didn't, they would lose their talent to the competition and their losses would become even greater. Some people complained that this was against the basic principle of paying bonus only when the company made a good profit. These people were soon silenced. That principle had long ago been abandoned already.

Distortion Number Three was that in the late 90's and early 2000's new recruits started negotiating "guaranteed bonuses". They argued that, in order to leave "Investment Bank A", where they had some deals in the pipeline and would probably get a bonus of $500,000 at the end of the year, they wanted "Investment Bank B" to guarantee them a bonus of $ 500,000 on their first year, to make it worthwhile to switch jobs. Some traders were so good at this that they switched jobs often, ensuring guaranteed bonuses each time and never having to make a single deal to deserve it! Incompetent managers made it possible, hiring swindlers rather than good professionals, and rewarding swindlers to become even better at swindling! To me, this is not a bonus. This is fixed salary, in disguise. You don't get it every month, only at the end of the year, but it is not linked to your performance, you get it just for showing up! When some managers objected, or a few rare HR professionals raised flags saying that this was merely inflating the compensation market for traders, they were pushed aside and told the same argument again: "if we don't do this, we will lose our best people to our competitors and we won't be able to attract talent!"

So what happened at AIG? By 2008, they had all three Distortions happily in place, plus Distortion Number Four: behaving like an investment bank, when you're supposed to be an insurance company!

In order to increase their leverage, AIG started investing their capital in unusual, riskier ways, and running hedges. To do that, they started recruiting from Wall Street, using Wall Street compensation practices.

The truth is, the 160 million are not really bonuses. They are fixed salaries in disguise, dressed up as bonuses. They are contractual. They are part of the labor contract just like normal salary is. The irony is that, if these people had insurance company pay packages, there would be no outcry... They would be paid competitive salaries (rather on the high side compared to what you would get as a consumer goods product manager) and nobody would complain. People are outraged because they saw the word "bonus". They think this is still linked to "having a good profit and paying awards to people who have contributed in an extraordinary way to that good profit". Sorry guys, but those principles are old-fashioned. They went out of style 30 years ago (although they were, and still are, sound principles).

The mob with the pitchforks and torches are at the gates of the wrong castle. They are chasing some guy for being ugly. This guy is not Frankenstein's monster, he's just ugly...

The real monsters are the ones who started all this and who distorted good pay-for-performance bonus schemes, turning them into inflated salaries disguised as bonus schemes. This means a lot of people are to blame. A lot of people contributed to these Four Distortions, to these "bogus bonuses" which are not really bonuses anymore.

Protesters demonstrating against AIG say that "AIG" stands for "Ain't It Greed". Yes, it is. But not the 160 million in bonus. This is just the epilogue of a long path of greed. Maybe the guys who got the 160 million were the ones trying to save the company, who knows. The greed, in itself, is not such a bad thing. Greed actually moves the American culture. When it goes over the top, it turns bad.

Too much greed is what made AIG collapse. Too much greed made Wall Street collapse. Too much greed will be the end of Capitalism. Capitalism is not bad. Savage Capitalism is bad.

The opposite of Savage Capitalism is not Socialism, it is Tyrannical Communism. We don't want either of those. I want an economic system based on merit, under which human values like ethics and solidarity are part of merit, just as important as ambition and innovation. There needs to be room for individual freedom, but also respect for the rights of others. We need a better balance between Individualism and Collectivism.

Gandhi had his list of "Seven Deadly Sins", which should be hanging on the wall of every CEO's office as a reminder, all over the world. They were:

Wealth without Work
Pleasure without Conscience
Science without Humanity
Knowledge without Character
Politics without Principle
Commerce without Morality
Worship without Sacrifice

The lesson here is that virtue is all about balance. The global economic meltdown was about Number Six (Commerce without Morality). The solution is not to decrease Commerce (which would happen as a result of protectionism) but rather to boost Morality and increase both, in balance.

Bonus schemes are good. But they should not represent more than a third of someone's annual compensation. They need to be equally tied to goal-achievement AND to appropriate behavior (such as ethics and cooperation). There needs to be some management discretion in determining the final amount to each individual or team (Yes! Team bonus schemes can be more effective than individual schemes. It works in team sports; why not use them more often in business?). Bonuses should not be only the result of a formula (they should be different from sales commissions). And they should be used in combination with long-term incentives (such as deferred-payment schemes, stock options, shares etc.).

Intelligent compensation schemes will be a key aspect of economic recovery. They need to be designed so as to reward desired behavior and to avoid distortions leading people towards the road to ruin. It's time we turn our attention to building a better world and stop with the witch-hunting. Let's drop the pitchforks and torches and get back to work!

8. Are We There Yet?

When my twins were seven we used to take them on a long drive (770 km) to spend a couple of weeks at the beach. By the time we did this three times, they knew what to expect (a long, boring drive), yet they still asked, after just 70 km of driving: "Are we there yet?"

Throughout the current economic crisis, I've come under the impression that the media has the same mental age as my twins had when they were seven... Although, from the very beginning, there were several news items announcing that "we are going into a recession, and it's going to be a long one", still, every other day I read about people saying that there are "signs of recovery" and that "the worst is behind us" (which means we are going to see it getting better from now on).

Forget it. Get real. The global economy doesn't turn on a dime. Not even the American economy is able to do that, although apparently some people believe it can. There seems to be a childish wishful thinking behind this, a desperate yearning to believe that everything that has gone wrong will suddenly disappear in a puff of smoke, like magic. If only!

I think it was in "MAD" magazine that I once read that "Of course psychoanalysis takes years until you get better: think how long it took you to get so screwed up!" The same reasoning applies. The Dow Jones index peaked in October 2007, a year and a half ago. It bottomed in April 2009, at 50% of what it was. I don't see why it would not take at least another 18 months to be back where it was (that means October 2010). Historically, it has risen to previous levels at least twice as slowly on the way up, comparing to how fast it came down. This means April 2012. Now there's a realistic estimate for you. It might take even more, but to expect full recovery before April 2012 seems to be just wishful thinking, an emotional response, rather than rational analysis.

I met a consultant in Peru last year who said that "Economics is a branch of Psychology". At first I thought he was exaggerating, but I see evidence that he was absolutely right. The idea that the economy is rational, or that people are rational, is an illusion, which I find, to my surprise, some senior people are still clinging to. Their attitude is so infantile that it actually proves the opposing point: that people behave moved by emotions more than by reason. That includes people's "economic" decisions. Professors at Harvard Business School and senile (sorry, I mean senior) editors at "The Economist" should take note. See also "Descartes' Error", by Damasio, "Animal Spirits: How Human Psychology Drives the Economy", by Akerlof & Shiller, and "Engaging Leadership, by Parker & Marlier.

The truth is that emotions drive every single decision we make. The "rational" decision is a myth. People cling to that myth because they have difficulty coping with and controlling their own emotions. A purely "rational" world has the appeal of appearing to be more predictable, controllable and safer. The irony is that this is a totally infantile, at best romantic, point of view... Behind every action we undertake, no matter how simple (like, for instance, raising your hand) there is an emotional will to undertake that action.

Every choice implies emotional consequences. Every "rational" analysis brings with it the emotional consequences attached to the available options. We would do better to try to research and understand emotions better, rather than to underestimate their relevance or pretend that there are situations in which human action is devoid of emotion.

People who are afraid of their own emotions (and of the emotions of others) tend to have difficulty in making decisions (choices) of all kinds. They use excessive rationality as a defense mechanism against being in touch with emotions. They create a fantasy world of pure rationality. They join NESA (NErds Society of America).

Fear (an emotion) and anxiety (another one) drive people to wish for a quick solution to their problems, including a quick solution to their economic woes. In this case, the illusion will lead to frustration, since economic recovery just does not work that quickly. Why? Because in a recession people become more afraid, more averse to risk, less willing to invest, less willing to spend. This hurts economic activity, which only gets worse. Fear of the recession becomes a self-fulfilling prophecy, as it deepens and prolongs the recession.

Recovery happens when more and more people become less afraid and more willing to invest in their own businesses, when more people choose a constructive attitude rather than a defensive one.

This takes time. Fear usually comes very fast into our consciousness. Losing that fear usually takes much longer than it took to become afraid.

"We have nothing to fear but fear itself" were Roosevelt's words about the Great Depression in the thirties. The difficulty is that reasoning alone is not necessarily enough to dissipate fear. Inspiring words are helpful, but inspiring actions will be even more effective. When people see others making money and being successful, that will do more to dissipate fear than any Obama or Bernanke speech. The media could help, by publishing more stories about the people who are making it, rather than broadcasting from "Gloom Central" all the time, or stating that the recession will be over next Monday.

The problem here is that fear sells more newspapers than hope does. So don't hold your breath. Be patient. This is going to take time. We've barely done 70 km and we still have 700 km more to go before we get there.

9. A Crisis Of Stupidity

The US & the EU have been struggling awkwardly to resolve the world's economic woes for three years now and what is most appalling is the epidemic of stupidity that has claimed thousands of victims among world leaders on both sides of the Atlantic.

A New Health Threat: The VSL-2 Epidemic

Only just recently scientists have been able to identify a freak strain of a virus that has been linked to the economic crisis that began at the end of 2008 and continues until today. The virus (named VSL for "Very Stupid Leadership) has been known for years in its milder form: VSL 1, which is as common as the common cold and affects many leaders. VSL-1 is easy to diagnose and to treat. The usual symptoms are narrow-mindedness and short-term thinking, often accompanied by selective amnesia (forgetting past mistakes or commitments made just a few days ago).

Treatment of VSL-1 affected patients is pretty straightforward, consisting basically of workshops and coaching. However, when treatment is interrupted after only a few applications, the symptoms usually return and blame is cast upon the treatment. In reality, the cure can only be obtained if one persists with the treatment systematically for at least a year. In some cases, up to three years of regular treatment are necessary before the patient can be safely declared to be free of the virus.

The form identified now is a different strain (dubbed VSL-2) and has some peculiar characteristics which make it far more dangerous than the previously known form:

1. The main symptom is a severe decrease in intelligence as in the ability to solve common problems. This can easily be verified by using IQ tests, which will show a negative impact of 30 points or more when compared to scores obtained before the infection. The main difficulty is convincing the subjects to take the test once they have been infected (see next item).

2. It is far more difficult to recognize and isolate in a laboratory, because it is accompanied by strong denial and feelings of righteousness
3. It affects especially leaders in senior political positions, policy makers and regulators. Apparently people under 30 are immune to it, and so are investment bankers. The reason behind the immunity of investment bankers is still a contentious issue among researchers: some say that it is a function of the nature of their activity, others say that it is a function of their age (most are under 30) or of their mental age (certainly most have a mental age well below 30). Still other specialists have even claimed that investment bankers are not really immune, they just look smart when compared to regulators who have been deeply affected by VSL-2.
4. The short-term thinking is not as severe, eluding first efforts at diagnosing it. VSL-1 patients think in terms of quarters, while those affected by VSL-2 have a management horizon of 12 months. The pathology is determined by the fact that the 12-month outlook is applied even to issues that require thinking in five-year terms (or more), such as economic recovery and managing government debt.
5. VSL-2 brings about selective blindness to economic data, especially unemployment data, and damages the perception of social unrest.

It's The Stupidity, Stupid

The main problem world leaders face right now is not political, it is the economy. However, the real problem beneath that, the root cause of the prolonged economic crisis, is the stupidity caused by VSL-2. Apparently the virus also causes leaders to avoid taking measures that are consistent and "go all the way" in a certain direction. Rather, they end up implementing "half-baked" solutions or "watered-down" compromises, which are insufficient to address the issues as, needed.

In the US, leaders struggled to decide for economic stimulus packages and "quantitative easing". Basically, they opted for injecting billions of dollars into the economy, when the need was for much more: trillions of dollars were needed in order to capitalize the banks, create jobs and allow companies to hoard cash (and be less dependent on the banking system). The chosen solution proved to be insufficient, but since it increased the national deficit (DUUHH!) politicians quickly shifted their attention to decreasing that deficit, rather than increasing to the point where it would actually have an impact in job creation. The situation now is that banks and companies have excess cash, but not enough to invest in production and expansion (creating jobs).

In the UK, conservatives blamed the crisis on the Labor Party (a smart move, before the virus affected them), won the election by a narrow margin and proceeded to implement a program of economic reform. That's when VSL-2 set in, and the program went off-track. Rather than cutting expenses intelligently, leaders made the cuts in all the wrong places, totally overcome by VSL-2 (poor bastards!).

These symptoms are quite similar to what I have encountered in private companies, where leaders affected by the common VSL-1 have made stupid investment decisions (spending on the wrong things) and later have reverted to cutting expenses indiscriminately, across the board (which results in cutting expenses in the wrong items). In both cases, rather than deciding to invest smartly or to manage expenses with intelligence, affected leaders choose the easy (and stupid) option of doing it across the board. Eventually they are replaced by healthier substitutes, when it's not to late to save the company.

Stupidity on one side of the Atlantic (US: spending badly, on the wrong things, and not enough, then reverting to expense-cutting across the board). Stupidity on the other side of the Atlantic (UK: refusing to invest in job creation and cutting expenses across the board). The VSL-2 epidemic has become a pandemic.

Continental Europe has also become affected in dealing with the Greek-Irish-Portuguese-Spanish-Italian-French crisis. Leaders have failed to inject enough money in the economy, have failed to commit enough money to bail out Greece and the other countries involved. Rather than issuing Euro-bonds, which would solve the problem in the long term, they are still debating as if the continent was still made of sovereign countries. The future lies in strengthening the European Union as such, but leaders affected by VSL-2 fail to see that.

Meanwhile, the investment bankers, who are immune to the virus, are playing the international financial system and having a ball! They pick targets each week:

IB1 - "Ok, let's do Italy next week, then Spain again..."

IB2 – "Not Spain again! There's more potential in doing a different country. How about the US?"

IB1 – "Not yet. Wait until we're closer to the elections, then we can really make a killing! Let's do France instead."

Up until now, China seems to have avoided contagion. Some say that their cultural DNA is immune to narrow-mindedness and short-term thinking, but there have been some signs of contamination. Can they remain immune or is it a matter of time? No one knows for sure.

The Cure

In the 80's, the band "The Cure" had a number of hits, one of which was the song "A Forest". Therein lies the remedy against VSL-2.

Leaders need to look at the forest, rather than the individual trees, to fight against narrow-mindedness. In Europe they need to look at Europe as a whole (including the UK!) and not at the outdated and obsolete concept of sovereign countries. In the US, they need to look beyond partisan divisions and local states interests, focusing on the American economy that stretches beyond national boundaries and spans the whole planet.

Everywhere, leaders need to think long term, as if they were planting a forest that will take years, maybe decades to develop. Someone once remarked to a man planting a tree: "Are you planting a tree? That's going to take years to grow and provide a return on your investment, in terms of shade, shelter or fruit!" To which the man replied: "Then I'd better do it now, rather than wait any longer!"

Until someone discovers a pill that removes stupidity caused by VSL-2, let's launch a campaign inspired by another "The Cure" song, called "Close To You". Let's each of us get close to a leader we know and let's try to help him or her fight against narrow-mindedness and short-term thinking. Let's do what we can to influence these leaders in a positive way, looking at the bigger picture. By helping them we will be helping society as a whole, both in the short term and in the long term.

10. Helping People Cope With Change

The attacks in Norway on July 22, 2011, were a tragic illustration of madness empowered in our modern world. They showcased just how crazy an individual and our society can both be, and they raise some important issues we need to face and manage going forward. And I do mean going forward, not going backward.

Power to the people?

We have all heard the mantras of empowering people, repeated endlessly in the egalitarian societies of Northern Europe and North America, and trumpeted across the globe as THE way to manage people in communities and in organizations. Never mind the fact that only 9% of the world's population live in egalitarian societies and 91% live in hierarchical societies; the egalitarians think they have it right, and everybody else has it wrong. It has come to the extreme of trying to impose "Northern" values on the rest of the world by employing military force.

The truth is, no culture in itself is better than any other. They are not "right" or "wrong", they are just different.

To each and every culture there are "positive" and "negative" aspects that must be acknowledged and dealt with. No set of cultural values should be imposed on another community.

For decades the Scandinavian model has been touted as a utopia by many media voices. The tragedy in Norway puts the spotlight on some of its shortcomings. The tragedy also raises important issues about the "right" versus "left" movements in politics and about leading change and managing integration in modern society, in all cultures.

Technological advances in communication (the web, social networking, mobile devices) have given enormous power to individuals. This enables people to find their friends and keep in contact, instantly, no matter where they are. This empowerment of the individual has been hailed by the individualistic and egalitarian media as the apex of "Northern" values coming to life, utopia becoming reality: everyone is powerful and free to express themselves as individuals.

The popular revolts in the Arab World have been hailed by such pundits as "Facebook Revolutions" and welcomed as a shift towards egalitarian and individualistic values, leaving hierarchical and collectivistic values behind.

However, we need to realize that social networking is not a value in itself. It is just a technology, and it may be equally used for evil purposes as well as for noble purposes. You can find your friends to conspire, to commit crimes against humanity, just as well as you simply agree to meet on Saturday night to have fun together.

Empowerment of individuals may not necessarily be a good thing, when it also empowers the crazies of Oslo and of Arizona, as well as the jihadists and Al Qaeda. The real issue is not "Facebook", but rather what is it being used for.

People have criticized the Chinese government for trying to control the Internet, but the issue all societies need to tackle is: how do you strike the balance between individual freedom and collective harmony? And how do you resolve the dilemma between equal distribution of power and respect for authority?

Every society has to resolve these dilemmas, and each has done so in a different way. That is the basis of the research and analyses made by Hofstede and the many social scientists who study culture.

Dark Side of Individualism

The dilemma between Individualism and Collectivism, as described by Hofstede, or between individual freedom and group harmony, has actually been approached by many philosophers throughout history. It is sometimes summarized as "my rights go as far as where the rights of my neighbor begin". Hofstede's research went as far as measuring exactly how far do societies go in terms of choosing between extremes, and he identified (through factor analysis) five dimensions of cultural values, one of which is precisely the "Individualism versus Collectivism" dimension.

Looking at that research we can see how 100 different countries score as compared to each other, and we can see that the cultures who most treasure individual freedom are the Anglo-Saxon, the Dutch-Scandinavian and the Germanic. These are also very egalitarian cultures, as opposed to the collectivistic and hierarchical cultures found in places such as Guatemala and Malaysia, to mention just two examples on the opposite side of the spectrum.

My point here is that extremes tend to be dysfunctional, no matter on which side they are. When you are sitting in one of those extremes, culture-wise, you tend to think that the other side has got it "wrong", while you have it "right". However, it is very important to look at the downside of these extreme cultural choices, as we strive to develop cultural values that will make our world a better place for generations to come.

Individualistic and egalitarian societies offer many benefits to individuals, such as freedom of expression and a sense of empowerment. They also value individual accountability and the respect of individual privacy. However, the downside is sometimes the isolation of individuals and a feeling of loneliness in the crowd.

The empowerment of these societies means that anyone is free to buy automatic weapons and "express himself" by shooting random people. Of course, no society deliberately endorses that, but we need to realize that distortions result from the values we espouse.

Whenever a madman goes on a rampage (Oklahoma, Tucson, Oslo, etc.) or when we suddenly find that an individual has kept someone as a prisoner in his basement for years (Austria, Germany, California, etc.), we ask each other: how could that happen? How could this have been averted? Why was this not detected earlier?

The answer lies precisely in the values treasured by these cultures. The extreme valuing of freedom goes overboard and the respect for privacy translates into "not noticing" that someone next door is keeping prisoners captive for 20 years. (!)

Similarly, a guy acts crazy, starts sending all kinds of signals that he is psychotic or a psychopath, but people around fail to see that, or fail to act on that.

People fail to see the signs, because they have been brought up to look at explicit communication, rather than implicit communication. They look for content, rather than format. While people in Guatemala and Malaysia (just to use my previous examples) have been brought up to strive for "group harmony" and therefore are keen on body language, non-verbal communication and implicit signs of expression, people in Scandinavia, the Us and in Germany disregard such signs and focus on the explicit content of messages.

People fail to act on the signals they perceive (if they perceive them) because of the respect for privacy and the unconscious voice that tells them "I am responsible for my own actions, not for anybody else's... this is none of my business".

And then disaster happens.

This "individual responsibility" taken to extremes leads to social isolation and even lack of solidarity. It breeds individuals who go crazy and turn against those around them.

The opposite example was shown to me recently in Singapore, where a Chinese presenter stressed the importance of "mindfulness" when leading groups in Action Learning. To my request for clarification, she explained that "mindfulness" is "an awareness of the people in the room, of the situation as it unfolds, being sensitive to what is going on". Collectivistic cultures (such as the Chinese) foster this "mindfulness" in everyone, since childhood. Individualistic cultures do not.

Best Of All Worlds

I am not saying that the Chinese culture is better than the Norwegian. Nor am I saying the opposite. Let's just stop advocating that this cultural model is better than that one. Let's start by becoming aware of our own culture bias and how it leads to prejudice. Let's start looking at the pros and cons of our respective cultures, and let's explore ways in which we could make them less extreme, in both sides of the respective spectrum.

Right after the Norway tragedy, BBC reporters where suggesting that Norway should "change its policies" regarding police not wearing guns and lacking surveillance and control of public spaces. These reporters did not realize that they were asking Norwegians to become more British, in terms of reacting to the incident as if they were British. They failed to see that they were judging the situation from their own cultural perspective, rather than trying to take an impartial stance or simply asking open questions and allowing the interviewees to express themselves freely.

Perhaps I am asking too much when I long for news reporters who refrain from pushing their own personal agendas as they broadcast from different parts of the world... That would show some real respect for people!

What I am asking for is for us to look at our values and to discuss ways of improving the way we teach our children the notion of "right" and "wrong", beyond what we were taught by the previous generations. Globalization means that we have the opportunities to explore and learn from all cultures. Globalization is not "Americanization", it means exploring the full spectrum in each cultural dimension and forging different futures for each community.

It does not mean moving towards a "single global culture", but it does mean tapping on the richness of exposure to all cultures, understanding where your own culture is coming from, and shaping your community's future.

Helping People Cope With Change

Life is, by definition, equal to change.

Human beings are quite complex organisms and, as such, they change a lot, they grow and develop a lot, even though they don't go through the same metamorphosis as a caterpillar turning into a butterfly. Yet, as people grow and change, they need to retain their sense of identity, they need to be able to still recognize themselves in a mirror, even though they have grown a moustache, changed their hair color, or both.

If people change too much, to the point of not recognizing themselves, physically and mentally, then we say they "go crazy" or "lose their mind". We are all a bit afraid of "going crazy" when we experience too much change in our lives. We all need to maintain a balance between remaining the same, keeping our identity, and turning into someone completely different, losing our identity. Not changing at all, means death. Changing all means madness. We need to grow AND keep our identity, maintaining that dynamic balance.

Learning is change (a form of change). Not all change is learning, but all learning is change. Whenever we learn something, we become a little bit different from whom we were before learning what we did. Yet we can still recognize ourselves as being the same person. We also need to maintain our balance in terms of learning, avoiding the loss of identity. We all have a certain fear of learning, as we have a fair of changing (too much). Keeping that balance is key.

When we look around at the world in 2011, we can see that a lot is changing everywhere. All that change requires a lot of learning, just to keep up, and all of this is very threatening (to our identities).

The more changes, the more threatened people feel. The paradox, then, is that change can trigger a conservative reaction. The more a person is exposed to change, the more this person feels threatened, and the more this person turns to conservatism in order to avoid change and maintain a sense of identity.

The more we challenge people to change, the more threatened they feel and the more defensive they become, fleeing from change towards the certainty of continuity. The best approach is to provide support for such people, strengthening their sense of identity. The paradox here is that people who have a strong sense of identity are actually more open to change. They are capable of managing change in their lives without losing their identity of feeling afraid to lose it.

We cannot stop change from happening and most of the time we cannot even slow it down. What we can do is help people strengthen their sense of identity by making them aware of their core values (which tend not to change). The better you know who you are, what you stand for, what do you want, the better you will be able to cope with changes around you without losing your identity.

Fear Of Change

The biggest obstacle in all this is balancing support and challenge, balancing the need for continuity to maintain identity and the need for change to adapt for new realities. On one side of the spectrum you have "progressives" who push for change, on the opposite you have "conservatives" who resist change.

This is a different dimension from being "right wing" or "left wing". Conservatives are basically fundamentalists, and the "clash of civilizations" between "West" and "East" is actually a misnomer... In reality it is a clash between conservative Christians and conservative Muslims.

Progressives have nothing to do with that. Progressives are about integrating religions and values to build a better future. Conservatives are about fearing the future and thinking that the past was better, therefore we should preserve it and try to return to it. Progressives are about "up, up and away"; conservatives are about "back, back and stay".

We need both identity AND change. We need to balance both in order to move forward without loosing our minds and going crazy.

In that sense, the craziness of Oklahoma and Oslo are a signal that, for some people, progress is going too far, too fast, too soon. That doesn't mean we should stop social progress. It does not mean we should stop immigration and miscegenation, it does not mean we should go back to the notion of "pure" races and Nazism.

It does mean that we must address the social discontents and misfits who turn to violence, that we must manage social change in such a way as to avoid that the Geert Wilders of today turn into the Adolf Hitlers of tomorrow. We need to acknowledge that the "Tea Party" movements all over the world are expressions of the fear of progress, and these movements, when not addressed, may spin out of control (even out of control of their own creators and leaders) and generate mass murder, genocide and even destruction of the whole planet.

In the US and UK media people talk about avoiding that "rogue governments" (Iran) or "terrorists" (as in Muslim terrorists) gain access to nuclear weapons or chemical weapons and wreak havoc and destruction among millions. I am equally concerned that some crazy Christian fundamentalist in Utah may do the same thing!

People who are afraid of social progress can be very dangerous, whether they pray in a mosque, in a synagogue, or in a cathedral. To avoid the madness we must turn to acknowledging it, recognizing it, understanding it and treating it. It's no use trying to control it by force, by imposing an Orwellian police state. We do need to address it through education (and I mean radically changing traditional education practices), through social and political debate, through innovative approaches and policies.

If we ignore the craziness next door, we run the risk of becoming their next victim, or worse: we run the risk that our children become the victims of the social craziness we did not address.

11. Brazil Management Style

Brazil is booming. So what can we learn from Brazilian business practices, particularly leadership?

Syncretism in Leadership

The Brazilian social culture landscape is a true melting pot, in which many cultures and races have really mixed and merged. As "The Economist" pointed out, "there are no hyphenated Brazilians", contrary to what is found in the United States. America is more of a mosaic rather than a melting pot. The "hyphenated Americans" reflect the fact that immigrants have formed ghetto communities all over the country. In Brazil there are just "Brazilians", who are the result of a long line of racial and cultural mixing spanning centuries. The result is some rather interesting blends, which have generated also some blended styles of leadership.

Odebrecht Story

A fascinating example is Odebrecht Engineering, the largest construction company in Latin America, which has expanded to become quite active all over the world. The company has a very strong corporate culture, which permeates the Odebrecht Group, including sizeable investments in petrochemicals and clean energy.

It was founded by Norberto Odebrecht in the 1940's in order to pay off his father's business debts, badly affected by the wild swings in pricing raw materials during World War II. His father was distraught and became seriously ill, no longer able to run the business.

In his early twenties, barely out of college, young Norberto created a company deeply rooted in his own ideals. He had been brought up by a German Lutheran tutor, hired by his family to provide a solid education where they lived, in Bahia. Norberto's character was shaped by his tutor's humanistic teachings: valuing "the human being" as the ultimate purpose of life. He developed his business as an adult with the purpose of dedicating himself (and the company) to working hard in order to satisfy the true needs of his business clients.

Since Norberto lacked the working capital to pay competitive salaries, he devised a clever profit-sharing scheme, which was quite advanced for its time. He managed to retain his talented staff by offering them autonomy (through delegation, decentralization) and significant sharing of profits. His relationship skills served him well not only dealing with clients and suppliers, but also in establishing a bond of trust with his key staff. At the same time, to keep things clear and well organized, he introduced "performance contracts" at every level of the company, naming them "action programs". In each "AP" target achievements for each individual were spelled out, plus the necessary resources to carry out the program, and the expected profits to be shared as targets were met. As long as the basic conditions established in the "AP" were met, managers were free to manage as they wished, though they were also held accountable for respecting the business values (or "business philosophy"), which were extensively discussed with Norberto at every face-to-face meeting with his staff.

Brazilian Model Emerges

As business flourished, Odebrecht became known for its high quality standards, something that could surely be traced to Norberto's German background. At the same time, this was combined with a willingness to take risks that other competitors would avoid. The so-called "difficult" projects, which implied engineering challenges, tight schedules or uncertain funding structures, typically scared off other companies. Odebrecht would "bite the bullet" and take them on.

In order to continue growing, Norberto realized he needed to expand his staffing aggressively. So he introduced another innovative aspect: he added training and development targets to each "Action Program". During a project managers would invest time and energy into developing young talent to become managers in their own right. A measurable output of every project is the number of people educated to the level of being capable of taking over a higher-qualified role in another project.

The Odebrecht style of doing business became a syncretized mix of German practices (high quality standards, structured processes), "Bahia" practices (relationships more important than tasks), plus a longer-term perspective (education), decentralization and profit-sharing. The end result was a unique blend, not commonly found in other companies.

The Power of Blending

Globalization has resulted in a more complex world, in which a diversity of clients require differentiated products, which in turn need to be designed, manufactured and delivered by a globally diverse workforce. This boils down to complex demands on the capabilities of organizations, which need to be more innovative and capable of drawing from a wide repertoire of leadership and management approaches.

Cultures like Brazil, and also many others in Latin America, Africa and Asia, are now able to reap the benefits of syncretism: a powerful combination of influences from many different cultures resulting in unique approaches. Initially the predominant influences came from European immigrants combined with the native cultures and in many cases also combined with the African influences brought through slavery in the 18th and 19th Centuries. Since the 20th Century, however, immigration has also become a global phenomenon, with immigrants to Latin America including many Asian and Middle Eastern cultures. Brazilians go to Japan, Argentinians and Uruguayans flock to different parts of Europe and everybody goes to America.

The leadership styles and management styles they are bringing with them combine the disciplined strive for excellence typical of Germany, with the engagement capacity of the Brazilians to mobilize energy. They combine the focus on results, typical of Britain, with the Latino skill in developing relationships. They combine the flexibility of the Middle Eastern with the conceptual strengths of Western Europe.

Changes are seen also at the highest leadership levels. Renault sent Carlos Ghosn (half-Brazilian, half Moroccan) to manage Nissan and lead a successful turnaround process, making him their global CEO afterwards. Inbev bought Ambev and also a whole team of Brazilian top managers who soon took over leading positions in the acquiring company and led it to become the world's largest brewer.

What all these stories have in common is the competencies of these leaders, who developed them under the influence of a diverse mix of management cultures: part North European, part Latin, part Anglo-Saxon, part Middle-Eastern.

The latter half of the 20th Century was dominated by American management models. It looks like the next 50 years will be dominated by blended models, and the sooner companies are able to understand these models and use them productively, the sooner they will rise to dominant positions in the increasingly complex world of the 21st Century.

12. Partnerships

A few years ago I was the HR Director for Banco Real, a commercial bank that had been acquired to become a part of the ABN AMRO network. At the time we had 23,000 staff and 700 branches.

Our CEO was Fábio Coletti Barbosa, an inspiring leader if ever there was one. Fábio is very charismatic, and his charisma stems from his authenticity. Fabio is not afraid to be himself, in any situation, regardless of who is with him. This includes sometimes feeling shy, or embarrassed, and acknowledging that, whether it is when sharing a table with dignitaries from powerful countries or speaking to an audience of 1,500 people. This authenticity immediately wins over anyone who makes contact with him.

I have learned many things from working with Fábio, and one of them is that he is not afraid to ask for directions. This contradicts a widespread male stereotype that cuts across many cultures: men don't ask for directions! Well, Fábio does, and that only makes people around him increase their respect and admiration.

"Asking for directions" means also hiring consultants, getting expert opinion, and engaging in partnerships. All of these will add value to your business, and that alone should be reason enough to engage in it. Yet, most managers, especially males, have this nagging feeling that "asking for directions", or asking for expert assistance, or forming a partnership with another company, are endeavors that somehow will damage your standing as a savvy leader. I guess there must be some sort of archetype that as a male you need to show complete autonomy, you need to show that you don't need anybody else, that you are capable of doing everything on your own, like Superman or George W. Bush.

Nothing could be further from the truth, especially in this day and age, when businesses are increasingly interconnected and interdependent. Charles Darwin stated that "survival of the fittest" was not equal to "survival of the strongest", but rather it was about "survival of the most adaptive to change".

Not that long ago (50 years or so) business success was all about competition. Whoever outsmarted their competitors, was quickest to market, and shut the competition out, had it made. Well, things have changed, as they always do.

As businesses become more and more complex, competing in a global marketplace requires mastering many different aspects which were not relevant in the past century, but which can make or break a business these days. The only way to master such complexity is by forming partnerships. This immediately brings know-how to the business which otherwise would take decades to acquire.

I'm not talking only about product design, and access to clients, but also about relationships with all sorts of different stakeholders, from governments to schools and to NGOs. These stakeholders were practically irrelevant to any business only 50 years ago. Nowadays they are key to the success of virtually any business.

It was different in the 20th Century

Back in 1996 I was attending a course for senior managers and we had as a guest speakers one of the members of ABN AMRO's Managing Board. From the floor came a question: "since information technology is becoming such an important part of the banking industry, shouldn't we form a partnership with a leading software company, like Microsoft, in order to develop new ways of servicing our clients?"

That seemed like a pretty logical question in the eyes of the 25 participants of the course, and the expected reply was that "yes, we're working on it." The actual reply, however, was quite the opposite and disappointed everyone in the room. It went "Yes, IT is important for a bank, but it makes no sense to actually form a partnership with a software company. Those guys are totally different from us! We cannot work in partnership with someone who has a totally different perspective from our own."

We were all shocked beyond belief... I guess that response was an example of the kind of thinking that was predominant in conservative business circles in those days. Some ten years later, the reality is that ABN AMRO disappeared from the global banking scene and that MB member is still looking for a job.

Meanwhile, at Banco Real, in the beginning of the 21st century, people were getting a different message. Ever since when the takeover of Banco Real by ABN AMRO was announced, Fábio gathered his management team and told everyone quite plainly: "we are acquiring a large consumer bank, one of the largest in Brazil, but we do not know the consumer banking business. We are basically a corporate bank, so we need to rely on the people of Banco Real to make this work." He proceeded to criticize those who had expressed arrogance as "the buying partner" in this joint venture. He exhorted all to demonstrate humility, because, indeed, the consumer bank would represent 90% of the new organization, and it was the acquired party who detained the necessary know-how.

All this began to shape a culture within Banco Real, one of not being afraid of forming partnerships in order to add value to the business.

In the year 2000, Fábio formed a small group of people around him to discuss how Banco Real could play a more significant role in the communities around it. In those days, in Brazil, "Corporate Social Responsibility" was barely starting; it was not yet a popular "buzz word". We started discussing things like Sustainable Development, what role could a banking organization play in terms of social issues like poverty, discrimination, giving opportunities to the handicapped, gender issues, and also in terms of environmental issues like pollution, the use of water, financing industries that were harmful to the atmosphere.

One of the first things we all acknowledged was the fact that we were far from experts in such matters. We were all knowledgeable in different aspects of banking: risk management, human resources, financial control, marketing. We were interested in sustainability as citizens, as concerned individuals, but we had little more to offer other than our desire to contribute to these issues.

The obvious answer to our predicament was... partnerships. We decided to seek out people who were knowledgeable about these issues and invite them to our meetings. We began to articulate task forces in order to turn some of the emerging ideas into concrete actions. And in each of these task forces there were people from outside the bank who played a role, partnering with the bank in different shapes and forms.

We had task forces engaged in diversity, in water usage, in recycling, in energy usage, in designing "green" banking products, in reviewing the physical facilities of our branches to make them more compliant to the environmental and social issues that we wanted to address. In each of these task-forces, different "outsiders" were used. We needed government approval for some of the initiatives we were about to undertake, sometimes from local, municipal, authorities, sometimes from Federal Government.

The side-street boys

There was an alley next to the Banco Real building, which had become a hangout for junkies, sex perverts and misfits. The staff and the general public never used the alley. They immediately saw these menacing-looking individuals standing around and people would take a different path to get to where they wanted. In the alley there was a side-entrance to the building, but that had been closed years before, because of security. It all contributed to make the situation worse: since there was no regular traffic of people, junkies used the alley to get their "fixes". They also used it as their toilet. Nobody wanted to go there, people preferred to take the other three entrances to the building, on the other three sides of the modern-looking skyscraper.

Fixing that alley became one of the first targets for our Sustainability initiative. It was something very concrete, and its very existence (the way it was) would discredit anything else Banco Real would want to do in terms of the physical and social environment.

Technically, the alley was a public space. It was not on bank property, it was a side street closed to automobile traffic. Anything we wanted to do required the involvement, approval or action of the municipal authorities.

In the old days, back in the 1950's or earlier, the bank would have marched a couple of senior officers into City Hall and demanded action on their part to "clean up" the alley. After all, that was the responsibility of the municipal authorities anyway, and we were taxpayers demanding our rights.

That would have been the old approach. Actually, it had already been tried a couple of times by previous administrations of Banco Real, with very limited results. The police would come suddenly and arrest everybody who was at the alley. A team of janitors would wash the pavement. Three weeks later, the same guys would be back right where they used to be, and the stench would be back to usual.

So we tried a different approach. We sought partnerships.

We went to the authorities not to complain, but inviting them to meet and discuss alternative solutions. We invited journalists with a reputation for writing about drug abuse and the homeless. We invited sociologists from non-profit institutions for rehabilitation. We asked staff members to volunteer for the task force.

We basically wanted to involve our staff members who would think of this as "a cause", not as a "job". We gave them time off from their regular jobs so that they could be on the task force. Heading the task force was one of our senior managers, but all other members were staff volunteers and "outside" partners who had a stake in the issue.

After many weeks of often frustrating debates, the task force began producing results. They proposed to turn the alley into a kind of "popular" public space. It would be easy to clean it up, but how could it be done on a sustainable way?

Instead of calling the police on the junkies, the rehabilitation institution came in. They talked to people; they offered help, free of charge. Some junkies accepted, others moved to different locations in the city. This was no rose-colored initiative, not everything was perfect. But it was better than beating people with clubs or throwing them in jail for two days. We decorated the alley with huge potted plants.

At the same time, we got City Hall to give licenses to vendors who would establish themselves on the alley. We had an espresso stand with outdoor tables, a flower shop, an ice-cream stand. We built a little stage and organized free concerts on Friday afternoons by street musicians. We provided park benches where people could sit, have their ice-cream, read, listen to the music. The alley became a meeting place. In a few more weeks, the place became a "trendy" spot. We opened the side entrance to our clients and staff, creating a steady flow of pedestrian traffic that were also potential clients of the stands.

The funds for all this were provided partly by Banco Real, partly by City Hall. Most of the work was volunteer work with no pay.

We engaged a nearby school on a project, which had been suggested by one of the journalists involved. It consisted of creating a stream of tiles on the sidewalk linking the Banco Real building to the school. Each tile was hand-painted by the school children. We realized there were not enough kids on the school to paint as many tiles as were needed (more than a thousand), so we invited the children of our staff to come to the building's lobby during a prescribed week and paint some tiles. Everybody got a kick out of this. Parents were proud of the tiles their kids had painted and would later point them out on the sidewalk, after they were set in place. "See that one, with the little red doll? My daughter did that one, she's only six!"

The whole project took more than a year to complete. Involving the right people took weeks. Getting them to agree on things took months. Implementing the whole thing took even longer. To this day, everyone who had a part in it, no matter how small, is very proud of having done that. And everyone learned a lot from the experience.

From the very beginning, the way the project was organized became a model for other projects in other areas. The task force involved in reviewing the usage of water began by engaging all sorts of specialists from environmental NGOs. These specialists provided a wealth of knowledge and suggested many different initiatives.

In parallel, each of the other task forces was engaged in similar activities. The "product design" task force came up with an equity investment fund with a portfolio of "green" companies. This was the first such fund in Brazil, followed later by many others imitating its success.

The "physical facilities" task force worked on accessibility issues: they made elevator buttons in Braille and moved the panels to a lower height so that midgets and dwarfs could reach them (in all branches). Wheelchair ramps were installed in all branches. Again partnerships were formed with NGOs and government agencies to determine priorities and to acquire necessary know-how. We learned from these partnerships that special furniture was needed in order to enable disabled people to use toilets, sinks, computers, and they were provided.

The greatest lessons for our staff were about partnering with people who were allegedly "different" from your regular banking business partners. Psychological barriers were broken to work with NGOs and with government agencies. Traditionally, regulators wanted to come into the bank and find out what bankers were doing, trying to catch them doing something illegal and punishing them for it. Bankers were keen to keep regulators away, as much as possible.

After all this, there were huge paradigm shifts. Regulators were partners in many initiatives. Rather than trying to catch the bank doing something wrong, they began advising us spontaneously before something happened. If a change in legislation was being discussed by lawmakers, they would come and tell us to adapt pro-actively to avoid getting in trouble. By the time new regulation was enacted and watchdogs came by, we were already compliant. We became "good examples", "model corporate citizens" sometimes used to criticize our competitors.

Initially, other banks were quite upset about our approach. They would come to us at trade meetings saying, "how can you work with that NGO? Those guys are the enemy! They are trying to hurt our business!"

After a while and a lot of explaining from our side, we manage to "educate" the industry. Soon other banks were doing similar things, each according to their own style. Fábio Barbosa was elected president of the banking association. He became a formal industry leader, legitimizing his stance.

Race issues

I was a leading a very contentious task force: the Diversity stream. "Leading" is perhaps a strong word. I was smart enough to engage a great team of staff volunteers who dove into this very emotional topic with a lot of energy. We soon had sub-streams and task forces for training and hiring disabled people; race discrimination issues; gender issues; age issues; we formed a matrix organization in which some task forces addressed all of these issues from the perspective of the HR function: a task force for recruiting, another one for career development, one for performance appraisal, yet another one for training and education, and so on.

One of our major efforts was to recruit more non-white people to have a staff population that better reflected the distribution of minorities in the population in general. For instance, in those days, less than 2% of staff was black, while in the Brazilian population 12% are black.

Once again, we asked ourselves: who can we partner with in order to shed some light on this issue? How can we get more black candidates to apply for jobs? (We new that the proportion of non-white applicants was very small; apparently, blacks expected to be discriminated against, so they did not even bother to apply).

The answer was: let's invite all the NGO's involved in black race issues to come in for a meeting, and let's brainstorm with them.

The meeting was quite something. I wish we had filmed it; this was history in the making. But, of course, we did not want to inhibit anybody, nor create a platform for radicals to "show off" in front of video cameras. Most of all, we were quite unsure about what the outcome of such a meeting might be. What if it was a flop? What if we were kicked out of the room? What if nobody came?

As it turned out, we had 34 people representing 31 different entities. Everything you could think of, from Evangelical Blacks Association to the Muslim Brotherhood of Blacks. Black Studies Association from Universities. The Black Socialist Movement. African History Institute. And so on.

I started with a presentation of what the bank was trying to do, and why we were asking for their help. I was feeling a bit uneasy, the only white male in the room, assisted by two white ladies who were part of the task force, and an audience of 34 very annoyed-looking black people.

After showing them a couple of slides, in order to encourage participation rather than a monologue, I asked them to talk to us about their experience with Banco Real and banks in general. It was like a dam breaking. Out came pouring dozens of stories about how they had been personally discriminated against, as clients, as job applicants, as credit applicants, just trying to open an account or paying a utility bill.

I continued with the presentation and at some point I showed them a slide with the current distribution of minorities among bank staff: only 2% of blacks, the vast majority in the bottom ranks, none of them at middle management levels and above. Gender distribution was equally appalling, embarrassing even. I told them we wanted to change that, but we didn't know how.

A huge discussion ensued, with everyone speaking at the same time; some suggestions were made, quickly drowned by harsh criticism from the different factions present. It seemed like this was going nowhere.

Then a turning point came about. One of the more senior people in the room, a tall grey-haired man wearing an African tunic and headpiece, who was also blind (from an illness he had acquired as an adult) asked for silence and stood up to speak. He had been following the presentation by listening attentively to all that was said, while a young assistant sitting next to him described each slide as it appeared on screen.

"Let us all take a step back for a minute", he boomed in a deep voice. "We know this bank discriminates against blacks, like all banks in Brazil do. The truth is, we all have our prejudices as well, we all discriminate other people for one reason or another. I speak from experience. When I still had eyesight, I was discriminated for being black. I joined the cause against race discrimination, I became a militant. Then I became blind. People around me started discriminating against me for being blind. I can tell you this is even worse. Now, here today, these guys from this bank have done something no company has ever done before: they showed us their staff distribution numbers. All companies hide these numbers from us. These guys are being open, for the first time. Plus, they got us all together in the same room. This in itself is an accomplishment! Out there, we are all enemies from each other. We are constantly fighting each other. And we never go to the same meetings. What we have here is a unique opportunity, and we have to thank these guys for creating this opportunity. We are not going to solve our problems at this meeting, but this can be the beginning of a series of meetings, and after many such meetings maybe we can do something productive. I, for one, am hereby committing to join a group of people who would like to join Banco Real in continuing to address these issues!"

Profound silence followed. I wanted to hug that guy (who I had never met before) and thank him for saving my life. But I held back. A murmur started to emerge. Then a feisty lady who had been very outspoken from the start also stood up and shouted: "Our brother is right! Let's stop bickering and form a group to continue discussing this! If the next meetings don't work out, we can always drop out later. Right now, you can count me in!"

A round of applause followed. I breathed again. I dropped the remainder of my presentation (still five or six slides to go) and took the cue. I invited everyone to sign up for a follow-up meeting, which we would schedule over the coming weeks. More applause, people stood up and started lining up to sign for the next meeting, others came to chat with me, still others remained in the room engaged in lively conversation. This went on for another half-hour, as if people didn't want to leave.

The task force met several times with the black NGO representatives. They came up with several useful suggestions to tackle the issue, such as recruiting in community centers, in churches, spreading the word that we were trying to fight discrimination and increase our proportion of black people. We got a lot of great applicants referred personally by some of those attendants of that meeting. A lot of progress was made over the following months and years, though I suspect the problems still exist, just not as bad as they used to be.

I was later interviewed by the editor of a Black Issues website. He asked me: "so why did the bank do all this? I suppose they saw the value in improving their image towards the public in general, and probably got more business as an outcome, right?"

My reply was "That was not the reason behind it. Yes, there were business results as an outcome, but the real reason behind it was that there were a handful of people who really believed (and still do) that this was the right thing to do. These people: the CEO, myself, some of my colleagues and the dozens of volunteers who are part of the task forces, these are all people who believe in this as a "cause". That's the real reason behind it".

Brazil's next Top Model

Banco Real became the most admired banking brand in Brazil, after a couple of years, according to independent surveys. It also became the leading banking brand in terms of sustainability issues.

In hindsight, I realize that none of that could have been achieved without the partnerships formed with government agencies, universities and NGOs (previously known as "the enemy").

It all happened because as a CEO Fábio led the way, often by example, showing key people around him that it was "OK to ask for directions". He gave everyone a "license" to go out and ask for help from very "different" people, who brought added value to the business. No one was ashamed of partnering with these "unusual" people, no one was afraid of creating relationships with "the enemy" (regulators, NGOs, academics).

This created a model that was quickly adopted by many different areas of the company, regarding initiatives that had nothing to do with sustainability. The lesson learned was: "we can partner with other organizations, even with those who we used to consider too 'different' from us, and create business value from such partnerships. This can be done through formal, commercial agreements, but also informally, with no financial exchange involved."

In later years, Banco Real formed many partnerships to create affiliated credit-card brands, to re-organize relationships with providers of services to the bank (consultants, outsourced calling centers, telephone-marketing providers, building companies who built new branches or provided maintenance work, all sorts of things). Innovative products were created, financing all sorts of consumer services, from travel to used cars and appliances, cash-flow management products were designed in cooperation with clients, "pay by phone" products were designed with telecom companies.

Partnerships became a household name, rather than "providers". Whenever someone comes up with a business idea, these days, the first reaction is: "great idea! Who could we partner with in order to take this forward?"

I left Banco Real in 2003 to move to Amsterdam. I left ABN AMRO in 2007 to go back to consulting. What I learned about partnerships in Banco Real during that period from1999 to 2002 has become invaluable to me. The last time I visited Banco Real, in 2008, the concept was still growing and being extended to more and more different areas of the business, and the bank was reaping the benefits from it.

13. Arab Spring Misread

The media in Europe and North America have been cheering the anti-government protests in North Africa and the Middle East as "a victory for democracy and freedom" and as "the beginning of a new era". "A New Arab World" read the headline in Paris. Before toasting to this "new era" and risking disappointment by the time 2011 is over, people should take things into perspective and try to understand what is really going on there.

Looking at it from a culture perspective, we should realize that what is happening is actually not that new, nor will it necessarily lead to transformational change. As early as the 70's, Geert Hofstede pointed out that, in "High Power Distance" (Hierarchical) cultures, changes in politics happen "by revolution"; while in "Low Power Distance" (or "Egalitarian") cultures such changes happen "by evolution". Research shows that Arab cultures score high on Power Distance (PDI=80). In the UAE PDI can be as high as 90, while in Egypt the researched score was 70. So we are definitely talking about High Power Distance (Hierarchical) cultures in North Africa and in the Middle East.

It's important to note that the toppling of governments by popular revolutions is not something unprecedented in Hierarchical cultures. On the contrary, it happens rather often. By doing so, the Tunisians, Egyptians and Libyans are not "becoming more American", or more "Egalitarian"; rather, they are confirming their respective national identities and their basic values, which are different from those found in the US and in Northern Europe. Basically, they are protesting against their governments, which have failed to cater to their basic needs and aspirations. These basic aspirations are not "to install an American-style democracy", not even "to choose their leaders in free elections"... Their basic aspirations are simply to have jobs that enable them to raise their families and give them a certain standard of living.

In a sense, what is happening in the Arab cultures is not very different from what has been observed in Latin America in the past century or two: strong, long-lasting government leaders facing revolutions that ousted them by force. The Americans even coined the derogatory term "Banana Republics" to label these Latin American countries in which governments were constantly changing through military "coups d'état". Perhaps the Arab cultures are going through a similar phase. They don't grow bananas in North Africa, so maybe the process is not linked to that fruit...

On the surface, the Arab and Latin American cultures seem very different: the external (visible) layers of culture are quite different. The traditional clothing, eating habits, music, religion and rituals are very different. The underlying values, however, are somewhat similar. Practically all Latin American, North African and Middle Eastern cultures are of the "Social Pyramid" type. Research has shown that they share high scores in Power Distance and in Collectivism (as the opposite of Individualism) and also in Uncertainty Avoidance (UAI). This is not anybody's opinion; this is the result of statistically robust research conducted by different scholars in these cultures over the past 40 years. Anecdotal evidence merely confirms what research has revealed since decades ago.

The Fake "Facebook Revolution"

The story in the media is a very enticing one: millions of youths, connected by 21st Century technology, changing the world for the better. A wonderful story, that most of us (myself included) find very attractive. A sort of "hippie revolution" of the New Millennium, powered by social networks. As the Brazilian humorist Jô Soares used to say: "the only thing that would be better than that, would be if it was true!"

The truth is that, indeed, technology has made it possible for people to communicate much more easily and connect constantly. But technology did not drive the revolutions, people with guts did that. The enhanced connectivity made it possible to organize crowds much more effectively in Cairo 2011, compared to Paris 1968. It's not just about Facebook, or Twitter, it's about the whole infrastructure of satellites, mobile devices and the internet. And this infrastructure works for all parties involved: for the freedom protesters and for the police force repressing them, for terrorists and for the military. The technology is available to all, and even though in Egypt the government managed to shut down communications among protesters for a while, there are so many ways around such blockades, and economies are so dependent on the continuous functioning of this infrastructure, that it becomes impossible to shut down protests without simultaneously shutting down all of society.

The technology, therefore, accelerated the social communication processes. In 1968, it took days to get in touch with youths at the Sorbonne and get the numbers necessary to fill the streets. This can now be done in hours, instead. By the same token, repression technology is also much more advanced: police use Tasers, high pressure water, they are better organized and more adept at mobilizing platoons than they were 50 years ago.

What have not changed are the underlying values. The values driving culture dimensions change very little over time, and in terms of national culture, 50 years is but the mere blink of an eye.

The cultures in Egypt, Tunisia, Libya, Bahrain, Yemen, Morocco, Jordan, Iraq, Iran and Saudi Arabia are still pretty much the same in terms of the underlying values, just like they also have remained quite the same in European and American cultures for decades. Mostly, the external layers of culture have changed; and it will be mostly the external layers of culture that will continue to change in the coming decades. The "inconvenient truth" in culture is that the underlying values change very slowly, even more slowly than the climate, because they are determined by the education of children. National culture values change only if the education of children changes. As long as families and schools continue to educate children in the same way, the underlying values of cultures will remain the same. As Belchior, a Brazilian songwriter of the 70's lamented: "we are still the same, and we live just like our parents did".

This does not mean that change is doomed. What it does mean is that change will happen according to the underlying values of each culture. Americans will continue to be Americans. Egyptians will continue to be Egyptians. And people will perceive others through their own cultural bias. We all see the world through the biased spectacles that were imposed on us as children by our own culture.

The Anglo-Saxons, the Dutch, Scandinavians and the Germans are all "biased" by their own cultures (like everyone is biased by their respective cultures) to see the world in terms of Low Power Distance, little or no hierarchy, flat social structures, egalitarian societies as an ideal; they also value Individualism and freedom, to the extent of abhorring government pretty much like the Anarchists used to profess in the 1900's (the Tea Party movement in the US is the prime example). No wonder then, that when they look at the revolutions in Egypt and in other countries in North Africa and the Middle East, they perceive them as shifting towards their own values of individual freedom and equality.

I must disappoint them by saying that kicking Mubarak and/or Gaddafi out does not mean that Egyptians and Libyans are becoming American or German. They want the current leaders to be replaced by other leaders, of their own choice, but they still feel that some people in society should have more power than others (hierarchy) and should be entitled to certain privileges that accompany the greater responsibilities these people are burdened with.

Authority and Group Harmony

What brought down the dictators in North Africa was not the pursuit of less hierarchy and more individual freedom, but rather it was unemployment and the high price of food. People in a "Social Pyramid" want a strong, "undemocratic" government, as long as the situation allows them to enjoy a satisfactory standard of living. It is the Americans and North Europeans who have issues with authority figures, not the North Africans. People in the Arab world did not protest for democracy, they protested for better living conditions. When the situation worsens, they will take to the streets and replace their dictators with other, equally strong, powerful government leaders.

"Social Pyramid" cultures are also, by definition, collectivistic societies. This means that people belong to "in-groups" who take care of them in exchange for their loyalty. Group opinion is more valued than individual opinions, and group harmony (within the "in-group") is a priority. When sufficient critical mass is mobilized, thousands quickly become millions, growing exponentially as we saw in Tahrir square. These millions may be crying out for freedom, but it is a different style of freedom. These people are not "Tea Party" advocates! They have formed one large group for the purpose of ousting the current leader, but they will revert to their usual group loyalties once the leader is replaced, and the large group will be fractured accordingly.

What we saw in Egypt was a fine example of a collectivistic society at work. As the crowds increased in numbers, more and more people raced to join them. The larger the crowds, the more people wanted to be part of that. And the way they handled the military was also a fine example of "Social Pyramid" values: avoiding confrontation, the crowds enticed the military to join them, to be part of the collective process. Also, the protesters had no problem in having the military take charge of an interim government (demonstrating respect for hierarchy). The issue was Mubarak and his allies, not the military per se.

A High PDI and collectivistic society does not mean that people enjoy being bullied by dictators; what it means is that people rarely voice their dissent individually (like they do in Individualistic cultures). Rather, they voice their dissent collectively, as a group opinion. Because they have a great respect for hierarchy, they will endure abuse from authority figures to a greater extent than people in Low PDI cultures; but there is a limit to what they will endure, and when that limit is crossed, people will gather in groups and not only "voice their dissent": they will actually make a revolution and topple government.

None of this is "bad", or "good". It is simply consistent with the culture values of those societies.

"North-Westerners" may be surprised, but in two years time societies in the Arab cultures will look very similar to what they looked like in 2008, before the global economic crisis. The leaders may change, and some superficial aspects of culture will continue to change as they have been changing. However, the deeper aspects, less visible and related to core values, will change very slowly. The way people are managed, relationships are formed, business is conducted and communication is carried out, will continue consistently with each culture's underlying values, and will only change over a longer time than we would normally expect.

Moving towards free elections in North Africa is certainly a change; there is no denying that. Looking at Latin America in 2011 and comparing it to 1911, anyone can see there have been changes. These changes, however, are more superficial than we think. The high respect for hierarchy is still there, much higher than in the US or Northern Europe. In the Arab World, a similar process is likely to occur: there will be changes; there will be more freedom. However, the basic values will continue to drive the way people behave at work, within their families, among friends, wherever they are. Changes in the political structures are much more superficial than we think, in terms of culture. The core values of a culture will only change very slowly, requiring a lot of patience.

14. Egypt Needs Time

Egypt needs time, and I don't mean "Time" magazine!

Last week, the New York Times and "Time" both ran extensive items on the political situation in Egypt. All these published items demonstrated a strong culture bias that completely missed the point about what is happening in Egypt and in other countries in North Africa and the Middle East. Transitions to democracy in hierarchical cultures need time and both the magazine and the newspaper (despite having "time" in their titles) failed to understand the time perspective.

They also failed to understand the nature of what is going on in Egypt and they failed to recognize their own cultural bias (please see my articles "Take Off Your Glasses" and "Arab Spring Misread") when describing events.

Misperception

The main cultural bias involved is that people in Anglo-Saxon cultures are deeply annoyed by what they see in hierarchical and collectivistic cultures, because it runs contrary to their espoused values of egalitarianism and individualism. The "Time" piece reveals that bias very clearly as it summarizes the misperception in the final sentences of a 7-page cover article: "To the extent that they can re-establish the main political dividing line in Egypt as being between military rule and civilian democracy rather than between Islamists and secular democrats, they ("they": Mursi and the Muslim Brotherhood) have a fighting chance of making progress in rolling back the authoritarian post-Mubarak state."

The authors fail to see that in a hierarchical culture like Egypt the military are supported by a huge section of the population, certainly by the majority of those who are better educated and those who have the highest income. It is the people who make the dictators; they cannot remain in power without support from the people. The military have been in power in Egypt for sixty years because they had popular support. Anglo-Saxon journalists are so annoyed by hierarchical societies that they become blind to what is really going on. They think Egyptians should behave like Americans or like Northern Europeans, but cultures are much more complex and more diverse than that.

To Anglo-Saxon eyes, the military in Egypt are "evil" and they should hand over political power immediately to "civilian" rule, which in their eyes means democratic and egalitarian. The actual reality is: "civilian" does not necessarily mean egalitarian or democratic, as we can see in Iran and in other countries as well... The problem is that, to Anglo-Saxons, authoritarian regimes are always "bad", "wrong" or "evil". The Anglo-Saxons are the ones who see the main dividing lines as being between military rule ("evil!") and civilian democracy ("good!"). They fail to see that military rule is desired by many Egyptians as the only way to maintain stability, order and security. In hierarchical cultures, strong and powerful leaders are preferred instead of "democratic" types. The Egyptian people have a different perception of the dividing lines in their own politics. To the Egyptians, the main dividing lines are indeed between Islamists and secularists; they don't see an authoritarian regime as being the main problem.

What is really going on

Egypt is making a transition towards democracy, yes. But the time perspective for that to happen needs to be measured in decades, not in months. Anglo-Saxon cultures are short-term oriented: they tend to think in days and weeks; "long-term" means anything beyond the next quarter. A political transition such as the one Egypt is going through will take a decade to complete, and the final outcome will look very different from what you see in North America and Northern Europe.

Just look at two recent examples that are often mentioned in relation to Egypt: Turkey and Brazil.

Turkey is a model often referred to, since it is also a Muslim culture, not too far away geographically. The military in Turkey have been in control since Ataturk in the 1930's, who was basically a benevolent despot as were Nasser and Sadat in Egypt. The military in Turkey are gradually ceding power to civilians, but this transition process is nearing its tenth anniversary and one can argue that they are still in control, behind the scenes. How could somebody realistically expect that Egypt would go through the same process in ten months rather than ten years?

Brazil is geographically more distant, but the underlying values are quite similar to those of Turkey and Egypt: all three cultures are of the "Social Pyramid" type, that is: hierarchical, collectivistic, more caring than performance-oriented, and with high Uncertainty Avoidance. Brazil was ruled by the military from 1964 to 1985. In 1985 there was an "indirect" election, in which Congress elected a civilian President. The first free democratic election happened only in 1990, and it was a democratic disaster. The winning candidate was Fernando Collor, a charming and handsome young candidate, cut out from the American pop-culture politician model represented by the Kennedy clan. Collor looked great on TV, had great speechwriters behind him and captivated millions of Brazilians with no experience in voting. He turned out to be the most corrupt President ever to take office and eventually got kicked out by an impeachment process before completing his second year. It was only in 1995 that another election was held and that is when the political and economic consolidation process really began.

In 2011 the world "discovered" Brazil as an economic and political force, but that process was almost 25 years in the making. One could even argue that the turning point for the Brazilian transition came during General Ernesto Geisel's tenure as President (75-80). He had announced that the transition would begin with his successor, and he was challenged by Gen. Sylvio Frota, a hardliner who opposed handing over power to civilians, which he considered "unfit and unprepared" to run the country. Geisel famously confronted Frota and his allies, threw them out of the Army and proceeded with the transition as planned, which meant appointing Gen. João Figueiredo as "the last General" President from 1980-85. Over the years, gradually civilians took over and democracy became a solid institution (though very different from the Anglo-Saxon model). Geisel was a tough authoritarian type who used his personal style to ensure democratic transition. Almost a contradiction, but it shows that the military can be authoritarian in favor of democracy.

My point is simply that popular revolutions are a romantic notion that never yield the results of their ideals in the short run; real change of this magnitude requires more time than most people would like, and even then the reality in hierarchical cultures will remain different from that of an Anglo-Saxon democracy. Authoritarian leaders can often serve the interests of the people better than a democratically elected crook.

Are Anglo-Saxon democracies better?

The short answer is: no! They are not better than other forms of democracy and they are not even necessarily better than non-democratic governance. We must all realize that there are deep-rooted cultural values behind our preferred governance models. These values distort our perception of what is best for any given country. What is good for the USA will probably not work at all anywhere else, with the possible exception of another Anglo-Saxon culture like the UK or Australia. Many Europeans do not perceive the US as being really "a free country", since there is a lot of censorship in America and dissenting opinions are quickly labeled as "unpatriotic" or "un-American". What is best for Egypt needs to be developed by the Egyptian people themselves, according to Egyptian values, without any outside interference.

The results of the presidential election first round showed that the majority of the electorate did not want military rule and they did not want Islamist rule either. The majority of votes were scattered among 10 candidates who represented more moderate political factions. The haste in holding elections earlier, rather than in two years' time, resulted in the military's candidate and the Muslim Brotherhood's candidate getting each of them more votes than any other individual candidate, simply because they were better organized.

Mursi won the first round with about 12% of the population eligible to vote; his military opponent had a little less than 11%. More than half the eligible people simply did not show up, and most of the voters who did, preferred "a third alternative", but they couldn't get organized around a single candidate, as a consistent political force: they needed more time for that. Haste worked against democracy: it favored the radicals on both extremes of the political spectrum. The masses of Tahrir Square were manipulated into supporting an early election, which served the interests of non-democrats.

When Mursi won the first round, by a narrow margin and with only one quarter of the valid votes, many rallied around Shafiq, the military candidate, on the second round, simply to oppose the prospect of an Islamist dictatorship led by the Muslim Brotherhood.

People outside Egypt need to realize that many Egyptians would rather have a secular society run by the military instead of becoming an Islamist State.

In a few years (perhaps less than a decade, but don't hold your breath!) the Egyptian people may develop into an institutionalized democracy cut out after their own values. The main necessary ingredient, still missing at the moment, is education. The country will need huge investments in education, persisting for many years, in order to develop a new generation capable of making informed choices among emerging political candidates.

Pelé was right

In the eighties, when Brazilians were protesting against military rule and campaigning for "direct" presidential elections, Pelé was interviewed and famously stated that Brazil was not yet ready for a democracy because "the Brazilian people don't know how to vote". He was almost unanimously criticized for saying that, since that statement seemed to endorse military rule.

Pelé was right in saying that Brazilians did not know how to choose the best candidates. Most of the people were kept in ignorance by a perverse political system that did not provide universal education and allowed for ignorant masses to be easily manipulated by politicians with selfish agendas.

However, the best way for people to learn how to vote is... by voting! The best way to create a mature democracy is by exercising the right to vote, as often as possible, in all kinds of elections and debates. Democracy is not only about voting, it is also about expressing different political views, arguing different points and engaging in debate. That process needs to begin slowly, accompanied by education. The earlier it starts, the earlier it will yield results, one generation later (yes, it's slow...). Pelé was wrong about the implications of his statement. People need to be allowed to vote so that they can learn how to do it, improving with each election opportunity. Not allowing people to vote only delays the process. However, people need to learn how to walk before they can learn to run. Making them run too early will make them fall flat on their faces. So the building of a democracy needs to go hand in hand with mass education.

As a nation, Egypt is doing quite well, under the circumstances. They have managed to avoid a civil war such as what happened in Libya and in Syria. They have elected a civilian president and the military are ceding power gradually. The best realistic outcome will be that Mursi and the military, working together, may continue this slow process until the next election, four years from now. Hopefully, a moderate candidate who better represents the will of the majority will emerge during the coming years and will win the next election, taking the process a few steps further. If all this is accompanied by dramatic investments in education, Egyptian society will continue to develop over the next decade and will create its own democratic model. This will create economic stability and will attract international investment to develop the region. It will be a bumpy road and a few setbacks may be expected, but if the elite who supported military rule can also support a gradual transition process to a more inclusive society, good things will happen. In an Egyptian way.

15. London Riots

The BBC and the NY Times say that people are "puzzled" and "trying to make sense of sudden outbreak of violence" in Tottenham in early August. I'm not sure if it is "people" who are puzzled or is it the journalists writing about the events...

It seems clear that what sparked the violence was the killing of Mark Duggan, a 29 year-old black man, by police officers on Thursday, August 4. The headlines on August 7 might have well been: "Police Violence Spark Public Outrage". Rather, the local media chose to under-report the incident, and also the reactions to it, until it became impossible to ignore the scale of what was going on.

If this had happened in China, I'm sure the headlines in the US and UK would have blared against government censorship of the local media, who was kept from reporting fully on the incident. When the same thing happens in the UK (or the US) what do you call it? Self-censorship? Are government officials actively involved in "giving a call" to media editors, asking them to "be careful not to over-react" or "blow this out of proportion"?

It's not just the censoring that we should worry about, it's the broader attitude of trying to ignore the seriousness of the unemployment issue, trying to sweep it all under the carpet.

Reports from London talk of people saying that "This country has changed. We've lost something".

DUHH! Of course the UK has changed. Guess what? All countries have changed. All countries have lost something. Or did they have it, in the first place?

The NY Times has reported that people ask, "where has common decency and respect gone?" Well, common decency and respect was not there, in the first place, as something demonstrated to all. There was racial discrimination for centuries. There was a class distinction between "the ruling class" and "the working class", also for centuries. These things, unfortunately, do not go away at the blink of an eye. And, in terms of culture, a decade is equal to the blink of an eye.

Blame it on the outsiders

It's amazing how, all over the world, there is this "knee-jerk reaction" to blame outsiders for all your troubles. Foreigners are the favorite "outsiders". It's a tribal reaction, to blame the outsiders. The funny thing is to realize that people in cosmopolitan cities like London, New York, Paris and Berlin, are all still subject to this type of tribal behavior. "Blame the immigrants" is the reflex reaction. Ironically, the "immigrants" are blamed equally by Muammar Gaddafi for what happened in Libya, as well as by Tory leaders for what happened in London.

Even the local residents of Tottenham have said that "these people who are looting and rioting, they don't live in this neighborhood".

That is one of the issues of our times: people move around. People communicate (Facebook, twitter, mobile phones). It's no use blaming the outsiders, in a global world there are no "outsiders". You cannot cordon off neighborhoods. Would you like to introduce Apartheid in London? I don't think that would solve anything, it would only aggravate the problems.

The fact is that when financial disaster struck in 2008, the Labor Party was blamed for it. The irony is that the crisis was caused by speculation gone wild among investment banks, run by people who typically vote and support the Conservative Party. So the conservatives caused the financial melt-down, blamed the progressives, then got elected to run government and quickly set about to implement a series of policies that shifted the impact of the crisis away from "the ruling class" and on to "the working class". This is not only ironic, it's also tragic.

Unemployment has grown tremendously and is likely to continue at high levels for years, because of the policies adopted by the Tories. Reducing government spending immediately increases unemployment, as any second-rate economist will tell you. More important, still, is where are the spending cuts directed. According to the BBC, programs to prevent crime have been cut harder than programs to repress violence. Is this just stupidity or is there an evil mind behind all this, manipulating politicians to ensure that they make the worst possible choices in economic and social policy?

Conservatives were quick to "do unto others, before they do unto you", so they blamed the integration policies. According to their views, the "outsiders" are simply "bad people", and the integration policies of the past decades have failed to turn them into "good people". The failed integration policies are blamed on Labor.

The case for real integration

Unless economic policies AND social integration policies are changed dramatically, the situation will get worse before it gets any better. The first step is to recognize how serious the situation is. The UK is not on the road to recovery. Unless policies are changed, they will continue to have an increasing negative impact on unemployment, and that will stir more social violence.

The priority of economic policies needs to shift towards job creation, even if it means increasing government debt. Creative policies are needed here. Think about Schumacher's book "Small Is Beautiful". We need to create millions of job opportunities for young and old. Unemployment turns millions of people into outcasts and turning to crime is just one step away, especially when figures of authority are demoralized.

Right now, the police are demoralized. They've shot innocent people more than once in the past three years and stood idly by while the riots spiraled out of control. The politicians are demoralized: the hacking scandal revealed more than hacking, it uncovered a web of corruption in which press officials and politicians exchanged money and bought favors from each other. The police are also involved in that web, and all parties are also guilty of trying to keep a lid on the whole thing, withholding evidence and delaying investigations. The Church has also been demoralized, most recently by accusations of pedophilia and covering up investigations about it.

David Cameron has been said to favor "a shake-up" in London police. I'm afraid it has to be more than just a "shake-up" and it has to involve other institutions as well, including Parliament, government and the Judiciary Power. The reform needs to involve private institutions too, such as media companies, and also the whole education system. We have a crisis of values, and this means the issue is broader and deeper than normally portrayed. It is still manageable, but it needs broad and deep action, not just your usual "panis et circensis" ("give them bread and entertainment, and people will behave").

Integration policies need to change in order to foster real integration. This means gradually shaping a society that is the product of all social forces involved. It does not mean turning the UK into a Muslim society, but it also does not mean turning all Muslims into Anglicans. What it does mean is turning the UK into a pluralistic society in which the diversity of cultural backgrounds is seen as a strength, rather than as something to be avoided.

Yes, this country has lost something. It has lost the acquiescence of minorities to social abuse. Minorities have been taught the Anglo-Saxon values of egalitarianism, individualism and performance orientation. Guess what? They learned these values and adopted them! They believed the people who told them that "all people are created equal", "freedom is an individual's most important right" and "all people should have the same opportunities to progress at work based on performance and merit".

Now, this country can gain something. It can gain the richness of diversity. It can realize the benefits of learning from people who are different from you. It can learn to show respect to all people, even to those who share a different religious belief, to those who come from a different ethnicity. It can renew its Anglo-Saxon values by ensuring that indeed society is egalitarian and does not privilege those who live in certain neighborhoods. It can ensure that individuals are held accountable, no matter how high in government their positions. And it can enforce the value of performance as being the criteria for progress at work, rather than sharing the same club with a government official.

The UK of the 21st Century will be perhaps more balanced in its values. It may evolve into a kind of balanced egalitarianism in which there are no longer distinctions between "the ruling class" and "the working class", yet there is still respect for authority. It may come to value freedom of expression in balance with maintaining group harmony. And it may temper performance orientation with quality of life and caring for others, so that people get a better work-life balance. The answer to its social issues lies in looking ahead, looking towards new solutions, rather than trying to return to the past. We need to respect and understand the past, so that we can avoid repeating it. We need to create a future that is better than our past.

16. Democracy In China

The press in the US and the UK keep bitching about the lack of democracy in China and in other parts of the world, notably in Africa, Asia and the Middle East. Recently, when totalitarian regimes (supported by the US, by the way) were overthrown in Tunisia, in Egypt and Libya, the press was quick to label it as the "Arab Spring" and hail a new era of democracy coming to Northern Africa. As other popular revolts began to appear in Bahrain, Yemen and Syria, again the press interpreted that as movements demanding democracy. Soon there were articles asking whether China would be next, or how long until democracy would begin to be demanded also in China.

None of those article authors seemed to be aware of the most important factor underlying all these different situations: culture. All those authors looked at the situations through their own culture biases, failing to be aware of that. And all failed to comprehend what was going on in North Africa, as they also fail to understand what goes on in China.

Even though Geert Hofstede published his first research studies in the 70's, many people still do not understand the implications and continue to ignore the influence of culture values in politics and in the way societies organize themselves. It may come as a surprise to those authors that other cultures do NOT share the same values as the US and the UK.

High Power Distance Cultures

A few years ago I was facilitating a workshop on managing across cultures for a group of people coming from several different cultural backgrounds. We were well into the discussion of the five dimensions of culture identified in Hofstede's research, and we were specifically dissecting "Power Distance". An American lady asked what could be done to remove the present rulers from power in China, in order to change the culture to a lower Power Distance Culture. Obviously, she didn't get it...

Power Distance is defined as "the extent to which the less powerful members of institutions and organisations accept that power is distributed unequally in society." Therefore, Power Distance (PDI) in a society is not determined by its rulers, but rather it is determined by the values of the people.

She still didn't get it. She argued that the rulers in China, enjoying absolute power, were manipulating the culture to ensure that it continued to be "high PDI". That is the mistake often made by people brought up in "low PDI" cultures, or should I say, the chain of mistaken assumptions usually made:

1. High PDI is "evil"
2. High PDI is created and maintained by the individuals in power
3. "The People" want their culture to change and become a "low PDI" culture

What this American lady failed to realize was that, in fact, high PDI is not "evil" per se. It is only perceived as such by people coming from a different culture. Conversely, people from China (or any other high PDI culture) might look at the US (or any other low PDI culture) and say: "How terrible! People show no respect for authority! What an evil, chaotic society!" They might even add "how could we overthrow their incompetent leaders and replace them with someone who earns the respect they deserve and restores the natural order of things?"

It seems that it is difficult to accept, in low PDI cultures, that it is not the dictators who define their power, but rather it is the acceptance of others who defines it. And yet, the fact that people accept a strong leader, with a lot of power, does not mean that they are happy with their **current** leader. They may very well protest and rebel against the current regime, and replace it with a different leader. However, the new leader will be empowered by the people to enjoy a high level of authority, just as the previous one. People in a high PDI culture are not necessarily longing for it to change into a "low PDI" one. Most often than not, all they want is a change in leadership, not a change in leadership style.

Understanding the "high PDI" mentality

People in high PDI cultures believe that some people have much more power than others, and that is just a fact of life. It is readily seen in all kinds of situations, beginning with the family (where the elders hold more power than their children) and extending to work, schools, public institutions, everywhere. Leaders, managers, bosses, teachers, all are authority figures. They have "ascribed power", through their positions, which is seldom challenged, rather than "attained power", which can be challenged (and frequently is) in "low PDI" cultures.

Along with that ascribed power, they have privileges and responsibilities. The people in that culture believe that these things go together: power, privilege and responsibility. Figures of authority have power and they are entitled to privileges. It is only fair, since they also have the burden of bearing huge responsibility. All decisions are made by authority figures. All responsibility lies also with these authority figures. They are in charge of taking care of their people.

"Até amanhã, se Deus quiser... João Francisco e a mulher. E os filhos que tiver!"

This old regional Brazilian saying, from the South, means literally: "Until tomorrow, if God wills... João Francisco and his wife. And the children they may have!" João Francisco was an army General in charge of protecting the border between Brazil and Uruguay. For almost 30 years (1893-1923) he not only did that but in fact ruled the region exerting extreme power. He was known for taking no prisoners in the many fights that broke out among Uruguayans and Brazilians who disputed the demarcation of the border line, the revolutionaries who challenged the local governor, and cattle rustlers who smuggled sheep and steers from one country to another (often these three groups were the same people). Such was the respect people gave him, that this expression became popular: nothing would happen without him willing it (and also his wife and kids). In high PDI cultures power is assigned to the position and to the family members around it. Family members do not need to earn respect; it is their right simply from being part of the power holder's family.

The "great responsibility" that goes with it means that anything that goes wrong is basically the power holder's fault and he/she has to fix it. The power holder is responsible for everything. The power holder also is responsible for taking care of the people who are loyal to him (or her). If someone is sick, or has an accident, the power holders need to take care of the situation. If the accident was caused by a reckless driver, it is up to the power holders to punish the person who caused the accident. If the roads were in bad conditions, it is the responsibility of the power holder. If the driver didn't have a driver's license, it is the responsibility of the power holder to ensure that people without a license are not allowed to drive. The power holder needs to have police on the streets, constantly controlling if people have the proper drivers license, etc. If a building collapses, it's because the power holders should have ensured that it was being properly built by people with the proper license/authorization.

This creates a rather comfortable situation, which helps to explain why these societies continue to function in this way. People with no power (or with less power) have no responsibility (or less responsibility). There is always "someone higher up who is actually accountable, not me!" And those "higher up" guys are entitled to privileges, in line with the responsibility they bear.

Years ago I proposed an "egalitarian" health care plan in the company I worked for, in Brazil. The existing health plan, which had five levels of increasing coverage as one went up the hierarchy, would be replaced by a plan with only two levels. The proposal was shot down. Why? Because "people expect to get more privileges as they go up the corporate ladder! How can you propose to take that away from them? This is what motivates them in their career progression." Less privilege in hierarchy was perceived to be de-motivating.

China will never become the US

In China, a high PDI culture, people have ascribed power, rather than "achieved power". Such ascribed power lies not only at the top of hierarchies: it begins with the first levels of hierarchy, such as policemen on the streets, teachers in classrooms, first-line supervisors in factories and offices. It is often in these lower levels of hierarchy where one finds the most common abuse of power. These lower-level power holders are the most sensitive to challenge and the ones who most often avoid such challenge by abusing the power they have. They are the stalwarts of a high PDI culture, not some evil creature tucked away in a palace at the top of the civil service hierarchy. Power in China is not exerted by a handful of people at the top; it is exerted by hundreds of millions of people in every rung of the societal ladder.

If Barack Obama magically replaced the Prime Minister of China, he would be totally powerless to turn China into an American democracy. This would not be because his fellow cabinet ministers would oppose it; this would be because hundreds of millions of Chinese would oppose it, from the bottom up.

Changing the culture would mean giving responsibility to the millions who currently have little or no responsibility at all. It means they would have no one else to blame but themselves, for the big and the small things alike. It would mean removing the privileges that every middle manager has fought so hard to get. It would mean changing everybody's role in society, not only in government, but also at work and in the homes. The complexity and reach of such a change is beyond imagination.

Will China ever become a democracy? Well, yes, it might... but not a democracy as described in the US or UK, with only two political parties who are in constant conflict alternating in power. A democracy in China is more likely to resemble the democracies you see in Latin America, in Africa or in other countries in Asia: dominated by one political party and a coalition of supporters, who remain in power for decades before a different party with its own coalition of supporters takes over and reigns for the next couple of decades. A democracy in which rulers enjoy more power, privileges and responsibility, than their counterparts in the Northern Hemisphere.

Right now, the paradox is that China has never been so democratic in its entire history (which, by the way, is four times longer than the UK's history and forty times longer than the US's). Never before have so many people in China enjoyed so much individual freedom of expression, equality of income and distribution of power... It may still seem very hierarchical compared to the US, but it has never been less hierarchical than in the past ten years.

It is likely to continue to move, very slowly, towards even greater egalitarianism. Just how slowly? Chinese slowly. The time perspective in the Chinese culture is longer than perhaps any other culture in the world. It is especially the opposite of what you see in the US and UK, where people think in terms of weeks, rather than decades.

When the Chinese say, "the US Dollar should be replaced as an international currency by a basket of currencies managed by the IMF", they don't mean "by the end of next year". They mean "over the next 20 years".

When they say, "China is ready to help Europe resolve their financial issues" they don't mean "by the end of next quarter". They mean "over the next 20 years".

The Chinese do have the ambition to rule the world, eventually. But they intend to do it peacefully, without firing a shot. They will do it through the power of their economy, their values, their culture. When do they expect that to happen? Very shortly: by the end of this Century.

17. Language And Culture

In America there seems to be a notion that language actually shapes values and culture, rather than the other way around... It should seem fairly obvious to most people by now, that indeed values are at the core of culture and they determine the outer layers of culture such as overt behavior, rituals, symbols and language.

The pioneer scientific research studies of Prof. Geert Hofstede, which revealed the role that values play in this process, are almost on their 40th anniversary of publication, yet the general public, and most of the press, remain quite ignorant of this, plus the fact that extensive research has been carried out throughout these last four decades, by many independent behavioral scientists, basically confirming Hofstede's initial findings.

Guy Deutscher has recently published an essay on the NY Times concluding that, indeed, language does NOT shape perceived reality, yet he fails to go beyond the general notion that "cultures are different". Deutscher expands on the notion that language limits the expression of certain concepts and feelings, mentioning a couple of examples illustrating how each culture develops certain terms which are difficult to translate to other languages and cultures. Perhaps the main difficulty he would need to address is the fact that he is trying to express himself in English, a language that imposes many limitations. (see Deutscher, Guy – "Through the Looking Glass - Why the World Looks Different in Other Languages" London: Picador, 2011)

English has become the most widely dispersed business language in the world, the "lingua franca" used by business people to do business across borders. Yet it compares unfavorably to other languages such as Portuguese, which enjoys a wider range of vocabulary and expressions to convey nuances much more precisely.

There are some obvious limitations of English which are frequently mentioned, such as the lack of a proper term to translate "saudade" from Portuguese (meaning the feeling you have when you "miss" someone, some place or some time), or the lack of a term to translate "gezelig" from Dutch (meaning a psychological atmosphere of togetherness, coziness and warmth when you are with friends and/or family). A couple of examples refer to the lack of proper translations from German, like "Weltanschauung" (a way of perceiving and approaching the world around you) or "Schadenfreude" (relishing someone else's misfortune).

Yet the limitations of English are more basic, such as the fact that there is only one verb ("to be") to translate from the Portuguese "ser" and "estar", which make important differentiations in Portuguese. "Ser" means "to be in an abstract sense, in an absolute, timeless and placeless sense, such as in Shakespeare's "to be or not to be, that is the question". By the way, this has been accurately translated into Portuguese as "ser ou não ser, eis a questão".

What about "estar"? It means, "to be" in a concrete, time bound, place bound sense. When I say "eu estou feliz", it means, "I am happy" here and now; I may not be happy somewhere else, and I was not happy yesterday and may not be happy tomorrow. When I say "eu sou feliz", it means I am a happy person, existentially, regardless of place or time.

This was once brilliantly illustrated by a Brazilian professor who had been appointed Minister of Education and was leading a wide reform of public education in Brazil. He was challenged by a TV reporter on certain aspects of this reform and whether those aspects were not contradicting some of his stances as a professor. His reply was: "eu estou ministro, eu não sou ministro!" Meaning, I am a Minister (in the time-bound, place-bound sense) now, I am not a Minister (in the absolute, timeless and placeless sense) forever, and I was not a Minister before. Such a statement can never be made in English without an elaborate explanation.

The distinction is made more important by the fact that "ser" and "estar" are both auxiliary verbs, just as "to be" is an auxiliary verb.

Similarly, Portuguese has two verbs "ter" and "haver" which are both translated as "to have" in English. "Ter" refers to possessing something, as in "I have a purse" or "I have an idea", while "haver" is more used as an auxiliary verb, as in "it has been a while since we have seen each other", ("há tempos não nos vemos"). This has been brilliantly simplified by the Americans as "long time, no see"!

This simplification of the language is a major factor in explaining the dissemination of English all over the world as a business language. It is much easier to learn simplified expressions in English than to learn the many complex nuances of Portuguese.

The economic factor, of course, is the other factor, perhaps most important: English was the language used by the British as they spread their culture across a global Empire, and English (or something quite close to English) has been the language spread through American economic domination during the second half of the past Century.

The question now, of course, regards the future: as China increases its role in world trade, will that be accompanied by a substitution of English by Chinese (Mandarin) as the international "lingua franca"? Probably not. It seems much easier for the Chinese to learn English (and they are already doing it by the millions) than for most people in the so-called "West" to learn Chinese.

The real issues that need to be addressed are the core values, which lie beneath the surface in culture. It is the different values that determine behavior, practices and policies, not language. The Americans avoided the core issues of culture in the 70's and 80's, just as Hofstede's research was beginning to make an impact in other parts of the world. Meanwhile, in the US, people were finding that "language shapes our way of thinking", so there was undue emphasis on avoiding certain terms relating to diversity issues.

That's when it became "politically correct" to use certain terms and "politically incorrect" to use others. It became "incorrect" to refer to people as "black"; rather, the "hyphenated Americans" were introduced in the language: "African-Americans", and later "Native-Americans", "Italian-Americans" and so on.

Also, it became derogatory to address adults as "girls" or "boys"... To most cultures around the world this politicization of the American language seemed a bit ridiculous. You don't find these aspects in other cultures.

The core problem of basic values was being skirted by focusing attention on a superficial aspect of culture (language).

It's like the old joke about the husband who comes home to find his wife cheating on him having sex on the living-room sofa with the next-door neighbor. So the husband decides to replace the sofa with a new one...

Rather than addressing the core issue (the wife and their relationship), the husband focuses on an accessory (the furniture).

Culture can only be understood (and eventually changed, which is a very difficult and long-term process) by looking at the underlying values supporting the behavior observed on the surface.

Hofstede defined these values as "broad preferences around one state of affairs over another, to which strong emotions are attached". His research has identified initially four dimensions of culture values, then a fifth was discovered in the early 90's, and now a sixth dimension has been identified in 2010.

These value dimensions reflect the way different cultures have unconsciously resolved six basic dilemmas of people living together:

1. Power Distance – The degree to which the less powerful people in society accept the fact that power is distributed unevenly in that society.
2. Individualism – Whether people should feel responsible only for themselves and their immediate family or whether people should feel taken care of by groups, in exchange for loyalty.
3. Performance (Hofstede called this "Masculinity", but such a label opens a totally different can of worms) – Whether a society values performance and awarding status to high performers, rather than valuing quality of life and caring for others.
4. Uncertainty Avoidance – The degree to which people feel threatened by ambiguity and develop mechanisms to avoid it.
5. Long-Term Orientation – Whether a society takes a pragmatic, long-term approach or instead takes a normative, short-term oriented approach.
6. Indulgence – Whether a society allows indulgence in the natural pleasures of life, or whether it restrains that in general and to certain places and times.

The issues in American culture are linked to its core values: the belief that power should be distributed equally among people; the incentive for people to feel responsible for themselves and immediate family, rather than being loyal to a group; the emphasis on performance rather than caring; the relatively low concern over ambiguity; the normative and short-term orientation; and the preference towards indulgence versus restraint.

It's important to realize that these characteristics have been researched with tens of thousands of Americans, many times, in many samples, compared with samples taken from other cultures. They are not the product of someone's opinion: they are the product of many research studies.

Most important is the combination of these characteristics, not the individual analysis of each dimension in separate. For instance:

the combination of Individualism and performance orientation says more about America than looking at these dimensions in isolation. By examining the research diligently, one can better understand America and have an intelligent discussion about where it is and where it wants to go in terms of national culture. Ignoring the research is just another way of avoiding the real issues that need to be addressed.

18. Culture Wars

Not a day goes by without us reading about some conflict going on in America: the Tea Party movement versus the Liberal Democrats, gun control advocates versus the National Rifle Association, abortionists versus anti-abortionists, WASPs (White Anglo-Saxon Protestants) versus illegal immigrants, Christians versus Muslims, etc. It appears that there are deep divides regarding certain values in the US. You could say that the Civil War (1861-1865) actually has not yet ended and that the "United" States are in fact not so united after all...

Part of all this is due to amplification by the press: conflicts sell newspapers, so the media picks up on these stories and magnifies them in order to increase readership. Yet it seems that the US has more than its share of conflict stories when compared with other parts of the world. The explanation lies in looking at the American culture.

I'm not talking about Hollywood movies and hot dogs. These are superficial aspects of culture, which are easily seen above the waterline like the upper part of an iceberg. They include symbols (like flags), rituals and heroes. I'm talking about what lies beneath the surface and is not easily seen, yet is the most important aspect of culture: its underlying core values.

Stay on the surface to avoid getting drowned

It is much easier to discuss what lies on the surface: those are things that can be observed and measured, while "values" are something more difficult to grasp. Hofstede defined values as "a preference towards one state of affairs over another, to which strong emotions are attached". The emotional aspect is key: when discussing the issues mentioned earlier, such as abortion or gun control, emotions flare up quite suddenly, and given the characteristics of the American culture, conflicts can quickly turn ugly and result in physical violence.

Because of that, politicians often try to avoid these issues, in order to avoid losing votes. That was largely Obama's strategy during the presidential election campaign: he positioned himself "above partisanship". However, he has been often criticized by his own supporters for "not being tough enough" with the opposition, or for "not showing empathy" with the American people. People get carried away by discussions about health care and avoid looking also inside themselves, in terms of their own values and beliefs, and how that leads them to certain political positions.

The real issues that need to be addressed are the core values lying beneath the surface in culture. It is the different values that determine behavior, practices and policies. The values of the American culture make it unique. If people would like to make America even better, then the best way to go about it is to understand and discuss those values and help their evolution and continuous development. That is what will take America into the 21st Century and maintain its leadership in an increasingly complex world.

American issues, not universal issues

There is a tendency in the US to think that the issues being discussed are universal issues, which are in everybody's mind, all over the world. Not true. The issues being discussed as a priority in Africa, Europe or Asia are quite different. Each community discusses issues that are relevant to their culture, and each culture is unique. Therefore, the relevant issues also differ from culture to culture, plus they are approached in different ways.

Ask an average American what "the American Way" is about and he/she will most likely respond mentioning things like "freedom" and "the American Dream". What is this dream about?

It's about feeling free, having the opportunity to become rich regardless of social background. Equal opportunity: everyone starts off with the same chances, on a "level playing field", so that anybody could win "the race".

And who should win? Not necessarily the strongest, but the most competent. It could be the smartest, the fastest or the strongest, or a combination of all that. In order for the competition to be fair, no one should have an advantage before the competition begins.

What about cheating versus "fair play" once the competition has started? Well, that is where things start getting a little murky... What is considered "cheating" and what is considered "being smart" begins to get difficult to separate, because of the cultural values described in the previous chapter.

The combination of "low power distance" (meaning there is less respect for authority), "high individuality" (meaning everyone has strong opinions of their own) and a preference towards "performance" rather than "caring" (meaning that "winning" becomes very important) and "low uncertainty avoidance" (meaning fewer and broader rules) is actually a recipe for frequent conflict.

In American society conflict is not avoided: it is accepted and considered as something that needs to be managed. Confrontation is a desired skill. The 4th and 5th dimensions only fuel the flames: "low uncertainty avoidance" means there is a tendency towards taking risks, and "low long-term orientation" means the culture is very "normative" (there is only one right way to do things, all other ways are wrong) and short-term oriented (we need results NOW!).

It's no wonder that in athletics, Americans tend to focus on sprinting (100m dash) rather than on the marathon...

Finally, the 6th dimension (Indulgence) means that Americans tend against restraint; so restricting the pleasure associated with competing (and the "rush" of winning) is not endorsed. Rather, the "rush" of winning is endorsed.

The issue of gun ownership is so typically American that it has become a stereotype. Foreigners expect Americans to own guns and to be "trigger-happy", they make jokes about that on TV all over Europe and Latin America. The gun issue is deeply rooted in the same values just mentioned: because of "low power distance", people perceive government authority as an interference on individual freedom; therefore, the idea of government controlling or forbidding firearms for individual is deemed to be "an invasion of privacy" and "an infringement on individual freedom". Both these arguments are considered ridiculous in other cultures, where there are no "privacy issues" because people are more collectivistic, and government authority is not only respected but even demanded, because of "high power distance". In the US, everybody is encouraged to be assertive since childhood and to "not take 'no' for an answer". So both gun advocates and gun control advocates are very vocal about their stances.

In America the emphasis on performance (instead of caring) means that a person with a gun is focused on shooting accurately, not on whether they will be hurting someone. In other cultures, where the emphasis is on caring rather than on performance, there are just no guns in use by the general population, and no discussion about it. It's simply not considered an issue. The idea of violence being unacceptable supersedes the idea of performance.

"Low Uncertainty Avoidance" means there are fewer, broader rules: the "Bill of Rights" is the reference, rather than an extensive and detailed Constitution such as the ones you see in certain parts of Europe and Latin America. Litigation is settled by jurisprudence and precedents, rather than by citing the law. Additional bills have great difficulty in getting approved by Congress. In terms of gun control, the legal discussion centers on the interpretation of the Bill of Rights, rather than on issuing additional legislation.

"Low LTO" means that both parties (pro and against guns) show little acceptance of a diverging point of view and discussions tend to be short-term oriented rather than focusing on what the implications might be over decades to come.

Finally, Indulgence again reinforces the pleasures derived from shooting (a feeling of power, of performing well, of winning a confrontation) rather than focusing on restraint.

The bottom line

All American issues can be boiled down to the underlying values of the American culture. The bottom line, then, (a very American expression, focusing on the final result rather than on process or how people are feeling) is that in order to resolve some of these issues there will need to be resolutions that address the underlying value dilemmas.

Gun control is not the problem. The problem is not enough respect for authority, excessive emphasis on individualism (in detriment of group harmony), excessive emphasis on performance (rather than caring for others), too much risk-taking; not enough flexibility to reach longer-term goals of social stability; and too much indulgence.

So how can culture be changed? The short answer is: with great difficulty and very slowly (as in decades and centuries).

The core values of culture, the notions of "right" and "wrong" are formed in early childhood, up to when a child is ten years old. Many psychologists would say even earlier, up until a child is seven or eight. That is when Americans learn how to be Americans, the French learn how to be French, and so on.

Therefore, a change in culture can only begin with a change in the way children are educated, within the family, at school, in the community. As Hillary Clinton famously said, "it takes a village". I think she may be wrong about a lot of stuff, but she did get that one right!

There is hope for change, but it needs to come from the way children are brought up, and that is not an easy process to tamper with. The Internet and mass media like TV may provide tools to reach everyone in a culture, but providing changes in content is a different matter.

According to certain accounts, the Board of Education, which oversees changes in primary school curricula in the US, is dominated by Texas... (not exactly a champion for change!). 46 States vote with Texas on all content issues. If that is true, then we're in for a long ride, cowboy!

And who determines the content available on the Internet? Considering the characteristics of the American culture described above (Individualism, low power distance, performance orientation, etc.), I cannot see any planned change happening in the next two hundred years...

Perhaps the only kind of change that could be foreseen is "unplanned change". That might come from increased immigration and increased exposure to different sets of values coming from other cultures, different from the WASP stereotype.

If immigration from Mexico and from other parts of the world continues to increase, plus more and more content generated from non-WASP sources becomes available, then maybe a different culture will emerge around 2200.

What will that look like? That is very difficult to predict. I hope it is a culture in which more people can be healthy and happy, more than today. That in itself would be an amazing improvement for our great-great-grandchildren!

19. My Neighbor For President

What did George W. Bush, Luis Inacio Lula da Silva, Evo Morales and Hugo Chávez all have in common? Pick the right answer:

a. They were all idiots
b. They were all dangerous
c. They were all incompetent
d. They were all "people like us"
e. all of the above

The correct answer is "d"; they were all "people like us". But if you picked "all of the above" I won't argue with you.

I find it amusing, if not alarming, that some of the most popular democratically elected leaders in America (North and South), were also so clearly unfit for the important roles they played. You can argue that, right now, Bush is no longer popular (the NY Times says 61% of Americans regard him as "the worst President of all time"), but don't forget that he has been elected TWICE in four years...!

Lula (also re-elected), by comparison, is still doing great! And he has enjoyed the highest popularity ratings, for the longest periods of time, on average, than any other Brazilian President in the past 50 years. Yet he can barely express himself correctly in his native language, has no decent education, and embarrasses everyone around him continuously with tirades like "my mother was born illiterate"... Quite a competitor for Bush's long record of gaffes!

I guess one of the paradoxes of democracy is that the candidate who gets the most votes gets chosen, though that does not mean he is the better-qualified candidate. The alarming pattern emerging from choices made recently (in the past 8 years) in the US, Brazil, Venezuela and Bolivia (please add other countries to this list, as you wish) is that people support someone they can identify with, rather than someone who they think is the best qualified candidate for the job of National Leader.

I vote on "Johnny Neighbor" not because he is the best person I can think of, but because he is somebody like me. Witness the popularity of Sarah Palin, and many other regional politicians in many places around the world. The "guy next door" type is a strong candidate in any election.

I think this means that democracy is in crisis; a profound crisis that is more far-reaching than the economic crisis the press enjoys so much talking about. People have felt "distanced" from their leaders somehow and have shifted their preference from someone they admire as "better than me" (but perhaps "too different" or "too far away" to respond to my needs and interests) towards someone "more like me" (and therefore more likely to "think the way I do").

Perhaps democracy has become a victim of its own success, and a victim of the fact that voters today are better educated than 50 years ago. People are less inclined to withdraw themselves from true participation and blindly "delegate upwards", fully entrusting their destinies to a "more capable" person. People begin to challenge whether their leaders are indeed more capable, if their leaders are genuinely acting towards the well-being of the overall population. And if their leaders appear to be "aloof" or "distant", then people prefer to choose someone who appears to be "closer" to them, even if less qualified than their "more distant" competitors.

The danger lies in that I end up choosing someone who is just as stupid and incompetent as I am, and I choose someone who is "friendly" rather than someone who is capable of doing a good job as a leader of my country. I sacrifice competence for friendliness. I end up choosing "Miss Congeniality" rather than "Miss Universe", confusing the criteria for the two titles.

In order to win elections, candidates need to balance their appeal between demonstrating competence and demonstrating "closeness" to the voters. This is what the "culture wars" have been about in the United States. Without the label, the same has happened in other parts of the world. A competent candidate will not get very far unless he/she demonstrates that he/she is "close" to the voters. On the other hand, "popular" candidates can get away with murder (and sometimes do).

"The problem is complex, and as such needs many solutions"... On one hand, candidates need to improve their balancing act to demonstrate both competence and "closeness". But on the other hand, voters have to continue educating themselves, and dramatically so. They need to become even more demanding, to the extent that they demand competent candidates and do not feel alienated from them just because the candidate has a different preference for vegetables.

The level of education in a given country has everything to do with the kind of politicians who get elected. Or, put in another way, "each country has the President they deserve". Better-educated people tend to vote for a better-qualified candidate. The danger therein lies in what will an incompetent President do once he/she is in office: probably not invest in education, because better educated voters might not re-elect him/her or the likes of him/her. Which leads to another paradox in democracy: leaders who have been appointed by ignorant people will try to keep people ignorant, to get a better chance of being appointed again. It takes a true statesman to invest heavily in education, also because it is an investment without short-term, visible returns.

Any idiot can see a new road or bridge, even if it is "a bridge to nowhere". Idiots cannot see the changes in the education system; often even if they can see them they cannot understand them and therefore appreciate them.

What can be done to save the future of democracy, when we see the terrible results of the US elections (electing a President who tried to impose democracy on other countries by military force – boy, did that guy get the whole thing wrong!), and the struggle in Europe to get approval of a constitution which nobody has read and everybody disapproves of?

Democracy needs to get back to its foundations: true representation of the will of the people, direct participation in shaping a community's future. As Michael Moore has pointed out (I know, he gets over the top sometimes, but sometimes he hits the spot) we have strayed very far from the sound principles of Greek democracy, in which:

a. small communities (cities) governed themselves;
b. congress did not consist of elected positions, but rather of people who were drafted and rotated every two years;
c. referendums were very frequent (several times each year, people voted directly on proposed legislation).

Politicians have argued that the increase in the size of municipal populations (and provinces, and countries) have made it impossible to have frequent referendums or to have the rotating draft system. I would argue that now, in the 21st Century, with the wide availability of the internet, it has once again become possible to have frequent referendums and rotating draft systems in place.

The thing is, our political institutions are still working according to 19th Century designs… Or rather, they are not working anymore. No wonder! It's about time we re-designed democratic representation, making full use of 21st Century technology so that we design 21st Century SOCIAL technology consistent with our times.

Joe The Plumber is not going to lead us in that direction (nor is Sarah Palin, Evo Morales, Lula or Chavez). We need people with a more modern mindset than that. (I know, "modern" has become an old-fashioned term, please bear with me.) The election of Barack Obama may be heralding a new era. Not only because of the kind of candidate he is (multi-cultural, multi-racial backgrounds, well-educated) but also because the use of the Internet played a major role in his election. This will change political campaigns everywhere. This hints at the direction we should be taking when re-designing democratic institutions. Obama will not save the world. But his election is part of a broader, global social phenomenon that politicians need to heed. Or get out of the way!

NGOs (in the broad sense, not just the ecology geeks) are the seeds for democratic institution re-designs. We need millions of groupings fostering debate and participation, to inform and educate ourselves, to raise awareness, political consciousness and responsibility. We need "Facebook-like" technology used to promote debate, to gather opinions and to actually count votes to decide on proposed legislation at all levels (communities, towns, cities, provinces, nations, regional blocks like the EU, Mercosur, NAFTA, the Arab League of Nations, etc.)

Democracy is imperfect, but it may still be the best (most fair) political form of government. But not the democracies we currently see in the US, in Europe or anywhere else. Democracy needs to be re-designed in order to recover its true essence and its added value to society. It needs to be re-invented and to move away from the jokes that we see around us, which, if they continue as they are, will only serve the purpose of fuelling terrorism and intractability among cultures.

20. The Commander's Choice

Here is an interesting case study. Apparently, it was inspired by the literary works of O. J. Simpson, who enjoyed mixing fiction and non-fiction up to the point that nobody could tell the difference anymore.

(Afghanistan, close to the hills of Tora Bora, early December 2001)

Captain Kirk: (entering the room) Sir! We have information that Bin Laden has been located not far from here! He is hiding with a few bodyguards in one of those caves at Tora Bora.

Commander Gallic: Are you sure? Can the information be trusted?

Advisor Heedlock: It might be an ambush...

Kirk: Positive, Sir. We have an insider who just came in. We can get him if we act now, Sir. He will probably move again in a day or two.

Gallic: Thank you, Captain. You can go now.

Kirk: Should I ready the troops and ask for reinforcements?

Gallic: No! I just said you can leave the room, let me think about it. I'll give you my decision in half an hour. Wait for my decision.

Kirk: Yes Sir! (salutes and leaves)

Gallic: (turning to Heedlock) Well? This could be the end of it! What do you think?

Heedlock: It's not that simple, Tim. Not that simple at all.

Gallic: Do you really think it might be a trick? An ambush?

Heedlock: You never know.

Gallic: We can get the area surrounded in 24 hours, probably less. We can start from the East, to cut his escape route to Pakistan. I can have 2,000 more marines here by tomorrow! Then we go in and squeeze him out.

Heedlock: Of course you can. And, by the way, I don't think there's an ambush involved, or that the information is false. He's probably up there, all right, because he has nowhere else to go. That's not the problem.

Gallic: Okay, I know what's bugging you. You don't want this to end so quickly. We just got you a billion-dollar contract to supply arms for the next three years. If we suddenly get Bin Laden and leave, you won't be getting any more contracts... You want this thing to drag on for ten years!

Heedlock: Tim, you have to look at the bigger picture... Plus, you have to think ahead, two or three moves ahead. Let's say you go out there and indeed you get Bin Laden. Let's say you get him over the next week or so. You surround the area, you start fine-combing. It'll take a few days before you eventually find the right cave, and, of course, he's not going to be there waiting for you drinking tea, is he? He will be hiding somewhere, but let's say after two more days you finally open a hole in the ground and there he is, like a boy hiding under the bed. What are you going to do then? Do you kill him? He'll become a martyr and inspire millions to fight against us. Do you take him to America for a trial? He'll be the darling of the media, all over the world. You'll give him a platform for his propaganda. Every jihadist on the planet will be out looking for someone to kidnap as retaliation. So what will you do?

Gallic: That's not my problem. I was sent here to get him and now I can do it. Mission accomplished. Let Ginfield deal with the rest. You're just worried about your goddamned contracts! If it were up to you, this war would go on for a decade. You just want to see it escalate and linger, the longer we're here, the better, the more money you make.

Heedlock: I'm not the only one who would benefit, Commander! You have a steady stream coming your way too, handled very quietly offshore. So your income will be affected if this is over and you pull out. Me? I'll be assigned to other contracts. There's a lot of demand in Africa. I'll continue to earn my bonus, just coming from a different part of the world. You're the one who will most likely end up in a desk job back home. I'll share the future with someone else who will endorse our weapons on the battlefield.

Gallic: I don't care. I'll get a bucket-load of medals for this. I'll be a hero. I'll get a promotion. I'll be known as "the man who got Bin Laden"!

Heedlock: That's exactly what I mean by not thinking ahead! You come home a hero; you're the guy who got Bin Laden. What happens next?

Gallic: I might go into politics, run for President, or something.

Heedlock: My dear friend, you're a Colonel but you have the stupidity of a General... You won't live to enjoy your fame! Every jihadist will be out to get "the man who got Bin Laden". The cruel ones will get to your family first, and save you for last. After what they've done to the Twin Towers, getting you is easy. Plus, they don't mind getting killed in the process, as long as they take you with them.

Gallic: I'm not afraid of getting killed. That's why I'm here!

Heedlock: Sure, but what about your wife, your kids? Should they suffer because you made a stupid decision to become a hero? Don't be so selfish, Tim. Besides, this might take months, years... Years of living in fear, not trusting anybody, afraid to walk the streets. Do you want your daughters to live like that? They'll never forgive you, Tim. You will ruin their lives.

Gallic: I have no choice. I can't go back now! They're waiting for my orders!

Heedlock: Of course you can. Tell them you need to consult Washington. Don knows what to do. He won't give the order. You're off the hook. The decision is not yours.

Gallic: What if this leaks out? What will people say?

Heedlock: I can guarantee there will be no leaks. I'll look after Kirk. Don't worry, nothing's gonna happen to him, but he won't say a word, trust me.

Gallic: But if Bin Laden crosses over to Pakistan, we'll never get him! From there, he can go anywhere. We'll never find him again. People will say we're incompetent.

Heedlock: Don't over-react. Nobody's going to say that, not even the Democrats. Right now, they're all supporting us. In eight years' time, with a new President, maybe there will be some criticism. Who cares? Some Congress committee might publish a report. So what? Eight years from now we'll both be doing very different things and we won't care.

Gallic: I don't know, this doesn't feel right...

Heedlock: Look, I'll make it easy for you: You've got two options. Option one is the selfish option, the coward's option. You go out there and get Bin Laden, you bring him to justice and everybody thinks you're a hero. A year from now they're still discussing where he should be tried, should it be here, in the US, in Holland, not to mention what kind of evidence can you really come up with. Who knows, he might even get off free, or die in prison waiting for a trial. Everybody's forgotten about you, except the Jihadists. Your life is hell.

Your wife divorces you, the kids hate you, you can't go anywhere without protection. You don't have a life anymore.

Gallic: Shit...

Heedlock: Option two takes wisdom and courage. The wisdom to realize that this situation is above your position, and the courage to admit it. You call Don, explain the situation. He will keep it quiet, and it's off your hands. He'll say that "the intelligence was inconsistent" or something. Tell Kirk that you received instructions from Washington, but they're classified. All you can say is that you need to wait. I'll get Don to move you out in six months; your time will be up by then anyway. The company won't let you down; we'll make sure your income remains the same, no matter what happens. You deserve it, Tim. You're an honest man and a dedicated soldier. You've served your country well for many years and hardly got any recognition for it. We will recognize you; we've done it before for many others who were less deserving than you are. And you get to provide your family with the kind of life they deserve too. Your choice.

In this fictional situation, the American Commander had to make a choice. What do you think he chose? What would you choose if you were in his place?

Note from the real world: on November 30, 2009, the Foreign Relations Committee of the American Senate published a report stating that in December 2001, although surrounded by American and allied troops, "Bin Laden and an entourage of bodyguards walked unmolested out of Tora Bora and disappeared into Pakistan's unregulated tribal area." "... calls for reinforcement to launch an assault were rejected."

On May 2, 2011, Bin Laden was captured and killed in Pakistan.

21. Fear Of Freud

Whenever I read "The Economist" (a magazine) I am struck by how "stupidly rational" their analyses of political and economic issues are.

I suppose this is because the people who write their articles are economists—people who have studied "the dismal science" and have chosen it as a profession. It seems that most economists are born with severe brain damage: they lack the right side of the brain, which handles emotions.

Sadly, they only have the left side of the brain, the rational side. Therefore, they have some serious shortcomings when it comes to understanding economics, politics, and life in general.

Adam Smith, a Scotsman regarded by many as "the father of economics" glorified the erroneous notion that "people are rational and self interested". Smith can be forgiven as a product of his era, the 18th Century. In those days science was still rudimentary. Yet, to continue to believe in that "people are rational" 100 years after Sigmund Freud demonstrated otherwise seems to be downright stupid...

The truth is that Economics is a branch of Psychology. It deals with human behavior and as such is influenced not only by reason, but just as equally by emotions and by values.

Economists should be required to study Psychology first, as a pre-requisite, and then study Economics as a Post-graduate course or specialization. Why don't they? It relates to a widespread syndrome, which I call "Fear of Freud" and which affect most people brought up in the Anglo-Saxon cultures.

The syndrome

This malady is easily recognizable by the following symptoms:

1. Fear of emotions; your own and other people's as well
2. Fear of expressing emotions and fear of dealing with people who express their emotions
3. Inability to express emotions and to handle situations in which emotions are expressed
4. Profound need to feel "in control" of oneself and of others

5. Belief that science is always rational and that issues which are not rational cannot be considered as "science"
6. Belief that reason is somehow "superior" to emotions and values
7. Denial of values as being just as important as reason and emotions

The malady is quite widespread in the Anglo-Saxon cultures, though in my experience I have often found it present also in Scandinavia, in large parts of The Netherlands, and also in some Germanic cultures. People in Latin America, Africa and Asia tend to be naturally immune against it, unless they have studied abroad.

The main consequences of the syndrome are that people make the wrong conclusions about all kinds of issues affecting business management, economics and politics. This leads to economic meltdowns, social breakdowns and political impasses, on a macro level. It leads to mismanagement, ineffectiveness and bankruptcies on a micro level.

Basically, people look for rational explanations regarding issues that are in essence emotional or ethics issues. They fail to find solutions because they are barking up the wrong tree.

Emotions and values are part of who we are, just as reason is. They all have equal importance in determining our actions, what we do, how we behave. Pretending that emotions and values are not at issue is simply denying our reality. We need to acknowledge their existence, their importance, and learn how to manage them.

Perhaps herein lies the difficulty, and the reason why we belittle and deny values and emotions: we find them more difficult to cope with. Reason is straightforward enough: it's logical, quantifiable, measurable, subject to demonstration. Emotions and values are not so precise; they are fuzzy and elusive things, which cloud our thinking.

Still that does not mean they are not important; it just means that they require more effort from us. More should be done at schools and at home to teach children how to express and accept their emotions. More should be done to teach people about the deep meaning of values, rather than repeating mindlessly whatever chants are being imposed on us by church and state.

So what is so frightening about Freud, anyway?

Freud started publishing his ideas at the end of the Victorian era, at the turn of the past century (1890-1910). That was a time when emotions were heavily suppressed, often denied. The supremacy of reason was all the rage. People who expressed emotions were regarded as mentally ill, or worse: devoid of virtue. All this emanated from England, but it was widely accepted as "the truth" in all of Europe and in North America.

Then Freud came along and said that people were basically motivated by emotions, which were primarily located in an unconscious part of the mind, which he called the "Id". These emotions were indeed unconscious, that is: people were not consciously aware of them, yet they were the main drivers of behavior. He explained that it was the suppression of emotions (rather than their expression) that led to mental illness.

Emotions were kept locked away in the unconscious by another part of the mind, the Superego, which harbored the values and the notion of "right" and "wrong", of what is "appropriate" or "inappropriate".

Freud described how basically everybody has emotional impulses coming from the Id, on one hand, which clash with the notion of what is appropriate or inappropriate (the Superego) on the other hand. The Ego is the third part of the mind, a part which is mostly conscious and rational, and which acts as a mediator in practical situations, deciding on whether it is "appropriate" or not to allow emotions to surface.

In practice, however, often the Ego is sort of distracted and it is the Id (emotions) and the Superego (Values) who are calling the shots. Our so-called "rational decisions" are anything but; they are actually driven by emotions or by our values, both of which we are only half-conscious of, at best.

The threatening thing about Freud is that, basically, he was saying: "you think you are in control, but you are not... your behavior is actually driven by emotions and values of which you are not aware!"

This, of course, challenged the accepted way of thinking at the time. What is worse: Freud said that most of our emotions are related to sex and violence. The "libido", or life impulse, and "thanatos", the death impulse. Bot these things were heavily repressed in those days. I'm sure that in 2012 Freud is chuckling in his grave seeing what goes on in the movies and TV: it's all about sex and violence, 24 x 7!

Still, in the early 20th Century, Freud's ideas were so threatening to the status quo that he was widely criticized, not only by the general public, who did not even understand what he was saying, but also by most of the "scientific" community. In a way, this only proved his arguments right: he was criticized out of emotional reasons and because of values. Barely a critic was able to provide sustainable rational arguments challenging Freud's ideas.

Freud was also a product of his culture (Austrian-German) and as such he was consistent. What he did was he provided an orderly explanation of the forces at work in the human psyche. He provided order where previously there was chaos. Still, these phenomena were so threatening to the prevailing mindsets, that most people could not accept this "new order" explaining what human nature was really about. They preferred to cling to outdated notions, much as scholars in the past had refused to believe that the Earth was not the center of the Universe.

One of the most frequent arguments against Freud was that his findings "were not scientific", because they were not the result of laboratory testing and could not be reproduced in a laboratory setting. This criticism stems from a culturally based and mistaken notion that "science" can only be considered as such if it is subject to quantified measurement and reproduction in a controlled environment.

Actually, "science" comes from the Latin word "knowledge" and the verb "to know". Somewhere along the line in history something got lost in translation... The word "science" was hijacked by the rationalists who dominated in the 18th and 19th centuries, so that instead of referring to any kind of valid knowledge (including knowledge about subjects which cannot be quantified), it came to be used in a more narrow sense, only in reference to the so-called "exact sciences", which were subject to quantification. We now know that this is a culturally-driven bias, though many people still believe in it as an absolute truth. Economists are among these...

The cultural bias

Our notions of "right" and "wrong", our values, our Superegos, are determined by the way we are brought up in childhood, before we are ten years old. This is basically culturally determined, and it has been measured and quantified by Geert

Hofstede and many others in the past 40 years.

What the research has shown is that the Anglo-Saxon cultures (or "Contest" cultures as described by Huib Wursten) have a bias towards rationality and against the expression of emotions. These are basically the cultures of the USA, the UK, Canada, Australia and New Zealand. These happen to be the cultures that produce the largest amount of literature on management and economics.

No wonder, then, that most economists insist on the idea of "rational man" in the analyses they undertake. These people fail to be aware of their own cultural bias, their own "collective unconscious", to paraphrase Jung: they are unaware of their collective Superego.

Small wonder, then, that most economists failed to predict the financial meltdown of 2008; they also fail to understand it to this day, as they fail to understand the issues at play with the Euro and with the weak economic recovery in the US. They are still looking for rational arguments to explain all this; they are still underrating the emotional and ethical factors behind what happens in the economy and drives human behavior.

Perhaps we need to put economists on the couch, to undergo psychoanalysis, much as Manfred Kiets de Vrees has done with managers and organizations in his own body of work. First in line for that treatment should be the editors of "The Economist". They have a negative influence on the public by disseminating outdated ideas to a wide international audience. They perpetuate the mistaken notion that people are rational. They underestimate the importance of emotions and values.

The world needs publications that are more holistic and unbiased in their approach. This would also make such publications more ethical, accurate and useful.

22. Pirates Of Talent Across Cultures

The war for talent in a global market has gone "nuclear". Although there is unemployment in North America and Europe, that unemployment has not made it easier for companies to find the talented people they need in order to be competitive in a global world.

As companies strive to become more efficient, more competitive, they try to keep the people who can drive that efficiency. They shed the others, those who do not have the skills to be top performers. As a global society, we are facing some complex dilemmas: the more efficient we become, on a global scale, the more we end up differentiating between "talented" people and "less-talented" people. We become efficient as organizations, but we increase unemployment by shedding jobs and the less-talented occupants of jobs.

If you look at these issues from a local perspective, thinking of your country as being your "world" or being your "market", perhaps the equation seems deceivingly simpler. At least the size of the labor and consumer markets will appear more manageable, counted in millions, and the boundaries of those markets seem clear.

However, when you look at it from a global perspective, the boundaries disappear and the whole issue multiplies in complexity and in numbers. The moral issue of efficiency versus unemployment also becomes more difficult to manage, from the sheer size of looking at a 7 billion people figure as the planet's total population.

If you are a business person, a government policy maker or an educator, you don't have to worry about being bored... But what can you do, in practice, to help your organization survive in such turbulent waters, and keep your own job from sinking in a sea ridden with pirates?

The Curse of the Black Pearls

As a company, your talented people are a treasure, on which your company's future is dependent. This treasure, however, is a living treasure. It needs to be nurtured as it is made of living creatures, not inanimate objects like jewels and precious metals. This living treasure can be made to grow and develop, making it even more valuable. Yet it needs to be protected from pirates, the talent-poachers from competing companies, just like you would try to protect a treasure of gold and jewels. Perhaps you might think of talented people as pearls: they can be cultivated or they can be sought out in the wild. And there are some that are very rare and very valuable: we'll call them "the black pearls".

If you are a talent manager in any kind of organization, you need to ask yourself some basic questions, in response to which you will need to make some initial decisions, or choices. That will be your starting point to go out in the world in search of the black pearls to ensure your company's survival.

Will you cultivate pearls or will you seek them out in the ocean (market)? There are pros and cons to both approaches, and in order to make your strategic choice, it might be good to lake at your overall corporate culture and business strategy, to make sure that your talent management is consistent with those.

In terms of corporate cultures, there are six basic types of cultures. Your specific organization may fall neatly into one of these six basic types, or it may be a combination of two or more of these types among the six basic models. The types are based on Hofstede's pioneering research on culture and its continuous evolution over the past 40 years (see "Cultures and Organizations" by Hofstede at al., 3rd Edition, 2010).

The "Contest" culture is typical of US and UK based companies. It emphasizes competition, internally and externally, it focuses on individual performance, measurable results, challenge as a way of motivating people, and financial rewards and prestige linked to individual performance. Since over two-thirds of management books are written and published in North America and the UK, most often people think that this is THE desired culture for any company, anywhere. Actually, it is not. American and British management practices may be very effective in their own markets, but they can be total disasters in other parts of the world.

The "Machine" culture is typical of Germanic societies (Germany, Switzerland, Austria and others). It emphasizes structure, organization and clear processes and procedures. The underlying assumption is that you have a well-designed and clearly communicated process; your company will perform excellently and be successful. It depends heavily on expertise for the design, communication and control of such processes, but once you have these in place, the system is practically foolproof.

The "Network" culture is commonly found in Dutch and Scandinavian companies. Its emphasis is on satisfying all its stakeholders. This means not only shareholders (return on investment), and clients (market share) but equally important: staff, suppliers, government regulators and the community at large. Maintaining this balance can be very difficult, but companies with this type of culture have become adept at doing that. Emphasis is not so much on performance, neither individual nor team performance, but rather on stakeholder management. There are huge implications on management practices, which may differ sharply from those found in a "Contest" company.

The fourth style is the "Pyramid", found in most companies based in Latin America, Africa and the Middle East (also some coming from Russia and Eastern Europe). These companies are more hierarchical in the way their structures operate. There are clear lines of authority, communication is "top-down". Business is done with an emphasis on relationships more than on tasks, internally and externally. Loyalty is essential. Leaders, at every level, determine the success of an organization or its failure, more than the quality of its teams or the expertise of its individual technicians. Again, huge implications for management practices, differentiating from the previous three corporate culture styles.

The fifth style is "Family", more often found in Asia. Very similar to the "Pyramid" because of its emphasis on hierarchy and relationships, it differentiates from the "Pyramid" because the informal organization is often more important than the formal. "Family" companies also tend to be more flexible and "ulterior-motive" oriented. Positioning in the market for the long term is deemed more important than obtaining profit in the next quarter.

The "Solar System" is the sixth basic type, and it is characterized by a significant tension between centralized hierarchy and the autonomy of middle managers. On one hand the "sun" in the system pulls planets to follow centrally designed directives, communicated in a top-down fashion. On the other hand, the "planets" (middle managers) re-interpret these directives and keep their own "satellites" spinning around them, each of them acting as king of his own hill. This type of culture is often found in companies based in Southern Europe (France, Italy Spain), but also in Poland and Belgium.

So, as a talent manager, the answers you may have to the primary issues of your function will be influenced by your company's culture.

If your company has a "Contest" culture, you will seek to identify the best performers as early as possible, who can deliver measurable results in the short term, and who are also the most confident and ambitious individuals yearning to grow and develop into larger roles. You may easily select a pool of talent among your broad employee base, perhaps just 5 or 10 percent of your total staff, and give them your total attention. Other staff members may yearn to be on that selected pool, but they are aware that there will be opportunities for them to be included, as long as they are committed to improving their performance and winning the internal competition to be selected.

If you are in a "Family" corporate culture in a Malaysian company, for example, it's a different situation and a different approach may be needed. Selection criteria may be influenced by relationships as much as by performance. The sheer ability to relate to clients and colleagues is more valued as a part of excellent performance, rather than the "bottom line" only, "hard facts" approach of a "Contest" culture. You are likely to put more weight on potential, rather than on performance, when assessing talent. Your very definition of "talent" may be different, to begin with.

If you are in a "Network" company and you try to select just 5% of your staff to be in your talent pool, you will face enormous difficulties. "Network" companies are very egalitarian. They reject the notion of choosing a small group to be outstanding. They reject the sheer notion of "black pearls" being more valuable than "common pearls", and they frown on whoever tries to stand out among the rest. Your "black pearls" will be cursed by their colleagues, rather than admired, and they are likely to be sabotaged and ostracized.

All I am saying is: be aware of your company's culture bias, as you start thinking about the way you wish to manage your talent; and be aware of the culture bias behind each of the procedures and tools that you are considering. Avoid using approaches that may clash with your corporate culture. If you choose for the clash, do so at your own risk and be prepared to dedicate a lot of energy to manage the conflicts involved.

Talent Management 2: Dead Man's Chest

As you progress in your talent management endeavors, you need to ask yourself about how you are planning to develop your identified talent, and even before that: what will you be developing them for. By that I mean: what kind of positions will be filled by these "black pearls" (whether you cultivate them or decide to find them in the depths of the ocean, I mean, "market").

You need a succession plan, in terms of identifying key positions, for which you will need to hire or groom talent to be ready when those positions become vacant, in the near or distant future. Think of each key position as a role whose current occupant will eventually "die"; that is: the occupant will leave the position, to take another position in the company or in another company, or to retire. For each person who "dies" for that position, you need to have a chest of potential candidates, identified as capable (or almost) of filling that position. For each key position you need to have a "dead man's chest" of candidates, hopefully with a few "black pearls" among those candidates.

Because, if you don't match your pearls with open positions, you run the risk of losing your pearls to the pirates. Your talent will leave the company to work elsewhere if they feel they will not get the opportunities they deserve.

What are these positions like? Are they positions that require occupants to be "a mile wide and an inch Depp" (I mean deep, sorry...), as generalists, or should they be "an inch wide and a mile deep" as specialists? Should you develop your talent to be generalists or to be specialists?

Again, corporate culture determines different approaches to succession planning, to career development and to matching positions with candidates. In "Contest" cultures you can keep people motivated through challenging projects, recognizing individual performance, providing performance-linked bonus schemes. People may remain in the same job level for quite some time (hierarchy is not so important) as long as they feel that their performance is being rewarded in a way that makes them feel proud.

In a "Family" culture, motivation is more linked to position (hierarchy), to the scope (responsibility) of the job, to how many people report to you. Motivation is also more linked to the importance you are perceived to have in the informal structure, rather than in the formal organization. This can be quite complex.

In a "Pyramid" culture the "dead man's chest" is quite clear to all concerned. There are clear positions in the formal structure. In a "Family" structure the formal position may be rather irrelevant. It is more motivating to be a trusted advisor in a "side" role close to Senior Management, than to be a Director in a role with no real authority or autonomy in practice. Managing talent in a "Family" culture requires more nuanced approaches, which may be more demanding for some people less comfortable with that kind of situation.

Generalists are easier to develop in a "Contest" culture. Successful performance is valued for its results, so a good manager needs not be an expert on a specific line of work, as long as he (or she) can deliver the expected results on the bottom line. In "Pyramid" cultures it is important that a manager demonstrates knowledge of the subject, since the way his department operates is more important than financial results.

At World's End

When your company is operating in a global marketplace, things get more complex and more difficult. You will have positions in different corners of the world. They will be occupied by very different people; perhaps by people coming from parts of the world that are different from where the positions are located. The criteria for measuring success will be different; the criteria for attracting and retaining talent will be different. Successful companies are the ones capable of adapting their practices to the different locations they are operating in.

Historically, "Networking", "Machines" and "Solar System" companies have done better at adapting their practices to far-flung parts of the world. The Dutch can be quite good at it, perhaps because they come from such a small country and have learned to do business "at world's end" centuries ago. Some argue that the Dutch "East India Company" was the first multinational corporation, established in 1602.

Others point to the fact that, in the Middle Ages, Holland was regarded by many as "the end of the world", being on the tip of Europe. Groningen, a village at the Northern edge of the Netherlands, was referred by the Dutch as being "the end of the world". Locals argue that, actually, it is not; but from Groningen you can see it...

The fact is that, by contrast, "Contest" companies have a scattered record in that respect. Some have been very successful as global companies, others failed miserably and had to retreat back to their home markets. Nowadays more and more "Contest" companies are learning to be more adaptable. Even McDonald's, once proud to serve the very same products all over the world, has in recent years adapted its menu to cater to different tastes in different countries.

When you manage talent "at world's end" you will need to adapt your practices, and perhaps make good use of the fact that young people are asking for international opportunities, more and more. Europeans and North Americans are eager to travel, to get international exposure, and to return to their home countries with that added experience.

However, when your talent is originating from a developing market (such as Paraguay or Pakistan), then often people prefer to continue their careers in the US or Europe, rather than returning home. This becomes a problem for those companies based in emerging markets and who perhaps financed the development trips of their "pearls", only to lose them before reaping the fruits of the investment made.

On Stranger Tides

The new, stranger tides, which we see in 2011, are due to the rise of emerging markets, which are increasing their share of the global trade flows, of the global consumer markets and of the global labor market as well. Europe and North America are still struggling with the financial meltdown of 2008. Asia, Latin America and Africa are booming and driving the global economy's shaky recovery. Young people all over have flocked to Europe and the US to get a better education, and have often stayed there to get better jobs, refusing to return to their home countries. Now the tide is changing.

The jobs in Europe and North America are scarce. Barriers to immigration are being erected, higher and higher. Opportunities in emerging markets are becoming more abundant and better paid, more competitive than before. There are also more continuing education offerings of comparable quality, with many American and European universities setting up campi in Asia, for instance. Emerging market companies are also becoming global companies, competing for leadership in the global market whether their head offices are in Sao Paulo, New York or Kuala Lumpur. These companies tend to have "Pyramid" and "Family" corporate cultures, and they are just as effective in the global markets as other culture styles. Their talent management practices are also different, but just as effective, as long as they are consistent with company culture and business strategy.

For a talent manager, managing talent "on stranger tides" means that you have to search for talent in all seven seas and be able to fight off the pirates in all of them as well. Companies are hiring Vietnamese engineers to work in Africa for Brazilian companies. How do you manage people from a certain culture, working in a different culture environment for a company based on still a different culture environment?

If you are in Malaysia, a young nation formed as such less than a century ago, itself combining Malay, Chinese and Indian cultures, how do you decide on your talent management strategy? Is your company a "Contest" company like the British and American companies, or is it more of a "Family" corporate culture, closer to the values found in the Malay, Chinese and Indian cultures? Or is it (probably) a combination?

You need to develop your own approaches, consistent with your corporate culture and business strategy. Don't feel compelled to follow a textbook produced in a different culture. Design your own models and adapt them when applying them in other countries. Use them daily and Knightley (sorry, nightly...) and watch your talents Bloom!

23. Six Visions

Six People In A Bar

P1: The world is a competition. There are always two opposing forces clashing against each other, and the outcome of that confrontation shapes the future.

P2: No, wait. That's a narrow perspective. The world is a series of forces coming against each other, not just two. The world consists of many different forces that interact constantly with each other and from that multilateral interaction different outcomes are produced.

P3: Hmmm... This sounds a bit confusing. The world needs order. Actually, there is an underlying order to everything. We just need to uncover that, we need to discover the patterns and further improve on them. As we find out how things are processed in the world, and as we bring improvements to those processes, we are able to better understand the world, how it functions and how it can function even better, to make it a better world for all, eventually.

P4: Sorry, but that's just too mechanistic for my taste... I think we need to look at the cosmos to understand the world. Planets orbiting suns, now **there's** a pattern which is reproduced everywhere, all the way down to the atoms, with electrons orbiting a nucleus. Human society also mimics that, with certain people acting as "suns", others as planets, moons, stars, and so on. Astronomy, if not astrology, offers a model to understand the world.

P5: My dear friends, I'm afraid you are missing the point. What matters in the world are human beings and their interactions. Forget about planets, forces, and other esoteric metaphors... Let's focus on people, and how they interact. Yes, there are patterns. They basically involve hierarchy, a sort of "pecking order". You see it in animals; you see it in human society as well. The individual is always part of a group, and in that group he/she has a place in its hierarchy.

P6: True, true... But this sounds a bit like a bureaucracy, a pyramid built by some technocrat with too much time on his hands and not enough sensitivity. Let's look at the basics again: the basic unit of human society is the family. Humanity consists of parents and children, who grow up to become parents of other children, and so on, forever. This is a natural process that has been there since the beginning of the human race. We are all part of a global family, consisting of billions of families.

What's Your Fancy?

The section above outlines (too briefly) six different visions of the world discovered through cultural research over the past 30 years, but not widely known outside the field of culture studies. Is the world a contest? A network? A machine? A solar system? A pyramid? Or a family?

The labels may be disputed (as all labels) but the visions of the world reflect the underlying values discovered by Geert Hofstede as "Five Dimensions" existing to different degrees in all cultures. Hofstede's "5-D" model has been the most widely researched culture model for decades and its practical use is gaining ground in global organizations trying to broaden their scope in a "flat", global marketplace. The five dimensions are: Power Distance (PDI), Individualism (IDV), Masculinity (MAS), Uncertainty Avoidance (UAI) and Long-Term Orientation (LTO). Over 100 countries have been scored on each of these five dimensions, so that each of these countries' cultures can be described in terms of the underlying values that help to shape those cultures. This leads to a better understanding of the cultures and their differences, but it still leaves us with a very diverse and sometimes confusing picture as we try to compare different cultures.

In order to help the understanding of the differences and similarities among cultures, the notion of "clusters" has been offered by Huib Wursten, Bob Waisfisz and others from ITIM, the institute that has sought to translate the outcomes of culture research into practical management applications. The six visions of the world mentioned at the beginning of this article stem from the six culture clusters resulting from different combinations of the five dimensions researched by Hofstede and other culture specialists.

I have found these six "mental images" very useful in looking at culture from a broad perspective. As you go deeper into a culture, you find the idiosyncrasies that make each culture unique, just as meeting people and getting to know them makes you realize that each person is unique. Still, the six images make it a lot easier to gain a broad understanding of culture differences. It also helps you to understand what the hell is going on around the world these days.

The contest – Cultures sharing these underlying values (low Power Distance, high Individualism, high Masculinity, low UAI) are basically those stemming from the Anglo-Saxons (ex: UK, US, Canada, Australia). In these cultures, the world is perceived as a clash between two competing forces (thesis and antithesis) out of which a resulting force ensues (synthesis). The fascinating aspect, to me, is to see how much this image actually shapes the way these cultures perceive the whole world, and not just the events in their own countries. It's like wearing color-tinted glasses and thinking that everything you see has that color.

"Contest" countries have two-political-party systems (Labor and Conservative in the UK, Democrats and Republicans), a mirror of the "two opposing forces" vision of the world. The problem lies in when this vision is then used (as colored-tinted glasses) to look at very different realities across the world. Then you get people saying weird things, like "Afghanistan will only find peace when it develops a democratic political system based on two parties". Why two parties? It's your glasses, mate! You don't really have to organize all the tribes in Afghanistan around two political parties in order to get stability in politics there...

The network – This is the cluster typical of the Scandinavian Region and of Holland. It shares low scores in PDI and UAI, high in IDV, just like the Anglo-Saxons, but unlike those, these cultures score low on MAS. The "network" countries see the world as a series of multilateral relationships in which many different forces come against each other and need to somehow be accommodated. Some form of consensus is required, and continuing monitoring of such consensus is necessary, for the process never stops.

They typically have multiple political parties and government needs to form a coalition in order to rule the country. When "network" cultures look at a place like Afghanistan, they come up with different approaches to the situation, like the "Dutch approach" of focusing on the tribal leaders and working with them to develop local governance and economic development, rather than fighting the Taliban. The Americans, of course, criticized the Dutch approach because it lacks the element of conflict, which under American-tinted glasses is the most important aspect. The Dutch wear other kind of glasses, so they see everything under a different color.

Which is the best approach? Well, the Afghan culture is neither a "contest" nor a "network" culture, so the answer is probably lying elsewhere... Don't try to rule Afghanistan as if it were the US, and don't try to rule it like Holland either!

The pyramid – These countries have high PDI scores, and low IDV. They are more collectivistic, rather than individualistic, and these cultures consider that it is simply natural that power is not equally distributed in society. Rather, some people have a lot of more power than others. In pyramid countries the MAS score is not relevant (in most of them it is neither very high nor very low). UAI scores are high, so they tend to be more religious, more superstitious, and they express emotions more often. This is probably the culture in Afghanistan (I say "probably" because there was no research yet carried out in Afghanistan. NOTE to UN: it would not cost too much to fund such research there, certainly less than a single bombing raid... And the research outcome would make all efforts to stabilize Afghanistan more effective!). There is available research data on neighboring Pakistan and Russia, which are both "pyramid" cultures.

In such cultures, the holders of power (like the tribe leaders), the groups to which people belong (such as the tribes) and the relationships among all these stakeholders are crucially important. Forget about equality. You need to involve the leaders. Forget about "taking individual responsibility" (this is the aspect in which the Dutch model also goes wrong). People expect the leaders to take responsibility, and they will follow them and be loyal to them, in exchange for being cared for. It's a different model, a different way of looking at the world. Change in Afghanistan can only happen if their view of the world is respected and employed in bringing about change. Get some people with "pyramid-tinted" glasses to come in and work with the Afghan tribe leaders. Then you will see things happening, at a fraction of the cost of the present campaign, not to mention the cost of lives, which is priceless.

The other three – The "machine" cluster is typical of the German and German-speaking cultures (such as Austria and Northern Switzerland); the "solar-system" is found in France, Spain, Italy; and the "family" cluster is typical of India, China and its "culture-relatives". I will not go into them here. I just want to stress that until we all are able to remove our "tinted glasses" or wear each other's glasses to see the world from different perspectives, we will continue failing in communicating effectively. The Americans will continue to criticize

Europe for being indecisive and lacking a single voice. Europeans will continue to criticize the US for being greedy and narrow-minded. The Arab countries (also "pyramid" cultures) will continue to criticize "the West" for meddling into their domestic affairs and doing more damage than benefit.

It's about time people realized that there is no single "right" way to manage neither an organization nor a country. There are at least six different ways (actually, many more, when you get deeper into it), all equally effective, each with its strengths and weaknesses. We all have our preferences, depending on our own background, depending on the way we were brought up. Putting ourselves in someone else's shoes is a step towards common understanding. This will help moving towards a second step, which will be to seek together solutions that make sense for both parties.

24. Bar Discussions Part 2

Six People In A Bar – Part 2

Joe: Let's start a drinking game!

Jan Kees: Why are you always turning everything into a competition? We don't need a game to start drinking... All we need is a discussion, and we are already discussing, so let's start drinking!

Heinz: OK, let's get organized: who wants beer? I will take note of what each person wants and I will get the drinks at the bar. Next round will be taken care of by Jean Pierre, who is sitting on my left, and so on, in a clockwise fashion.

Zé Pedro: My dear friends, let's not argue about something so pleasant as drinking among friends. Go ahead and order beer for everyone, Heinz. I have something to talk about with all of you, I need your help.

Jean Pierre: That's fine, Zé Pedro, but I want an Amstel beer, not a Heineken, Heinz.

Hu Tan: It's the same thing, Jean Pierre. Heineken bought Amstel years ago and they've changed the formula, now Amstel tastes the same as Heineken.

Jean Pierre: Maybe it's the same to you, but not to me! Heinz, get me an Amstel, not Heineken!

Zé Pedro: Enough with the discussion, guys. I've been asked to write an article about "Leadership" and I don't know where to start... Any ideas?

Jean Pierre: That "leadership" stuff is bullshit! We don't even have a word for it in French... It's just another American stupid idea. Somebody says "leadership" and suddenly the whole world is following the Americans without understanding what they are talking about.

Joe: I'll tell you something about leadership: it's about taking action! You know why there's no word for "leadership" in French? It's because the French are still discussing about whether there should be a word for it or not, and what kind of definition should there be, and is it a noun or a verb, and so on! Meanwhile the Americans are just doing it!

Jan Kees: According to me, leadership should be a rotating function in a team. Everyone should have a chance to be a leader, depending on the situation. The leader should not be always the same person.

Jean Pierre: What do you mean "according to me"? What is this, "Dutchlish" again? Just state your opinion, say "I think..." and so on and so on!

Jan Kees: I will drop the "Dutchlish" when you drop your accent, OK? Hu, what do you think? Give us an oriental perspective.

Hu Tan: Lao Tse said: "In order to lead a people, walk behind them!"

Joe: That's weird!... How can you lead anybody if you're not in front of them? You have to be out in front, in order to face the challenges, bite the bullets, make the decisions and show the way! You can't do that from behind...

Hu Tan: Both these things are true... They are not mutually exclusive.

Jan Kees: Hmmm... I don't know... They look mutually exclusive in my opinion. You either lead from the front or from the back, so what is your position? It looks like a dilemma to me. Where is Heinz? He didn't say what he thinks...

Zé Pedro: He is still getting the beers... Maybe he needs help. I will go and help him. (leaves and goes to the bar)

Jean Pierre: We were having the discussion for his sake, and then he leaves...

Jan Kees: I think a leader should understand three things: that we are all in a situation together, that you need to be frank and honest with yourself and with the people around you, and that...

Heinz: (interrupting) Here we are, six beers! They didn't have Amstel or Heineken, so I got Jupiler for everyone.

Zé Pedro: It's not bad; it's my boss's favorite beer.

Heinz: Now we can start the discussion.

Joe: We've already started! We're way ahead of you...

Jan Kees: I didn't finish what I was saying! I think a leader should understand three things: that we are all in a situation together, that you need to be frank and honest with yourself and with the people around you, and that you need to communicate a vision.

Jean Pierre: That sounds very Dutch to me...

Jan Kees: It can be very Dutch and it can also be very right!

Heinz: It's better if each of us gives our definition of leadership, speaking one at a time, with no interruption. Everyone else should listen, until we finish going around the table.

Zé Pedro: That's fine by me; I'll go along with that.

Joe: Anything, as long as we move! Let's get on with it.

Heinz: Wait! Let's do something creative, now: let's go counter-clockwise!

Jean Pierre: (rolling his eyes) Beautiful, Heinz! OK: Hu, you start. What is leadership?

Hu Tan: Maybe the question should be: "How is leadership?"...

Joe: Oh, great! Answer a question with another question!...

Heinz: No interruptions! Mr. Tan, do you want to say anything more?

Hu Tan: The worst deaf is the one who refuses to listen...

Heinz: Thank you. Mr. Poireau, it is now your turn.

Jean Pierre: The concept of leadership actually comes from the middle ages, when horse-drawn coaches were traveling along the countryside in Brittany and other parts of France, at a time when a portion of France was unduly occupied by English invaders, before Jean D'Arc defeated them at the battle of Orleans and later helped the Dauphin to become the rightful king of France. In those days...

Joe: Will you come to the point?!

Heinz: No interruptions!

Jean Pierre: (rolling his eyes again) ... In those days it was common for the coach to be driven by someone who was called a "manager", his job was, in French *"manager les chevaux"*, that is: to handle the horses. He would steer the horses, take care of them when the coach stopped for the night at a roadside inn, feed them, brush their hide, prepare them in the next morning to continue the trip, etc. This French verb *"manager"* (in English: to handle) was wrongly adopted, or adapted, by the English as a noun, meaning "the administrator", or "manager". The person in charge of ensuring that the horses are properly treated and that the coach is going along the way that it is supposed to go.

Joe: What's that got to do with leadership? Come to the damn point!

Heinz: Mr. Peartree, no interruptions! Carry on, Mr. Poireau.

Jean Pierre: (rolling his eyes again and sighing deeply) ... *D'abord,* it was usual that the coach was not traveling alone, only with its passengers. There were usually one or two other horsemen, maybe more, who traveled with the coach. They could protect the passengers against highway robbers, go for help if the coach broke down, all kinds of things.

(Joe taps his fingers on the table impatiently; Heinz gives him an annoyed look; Jean Pierre pretends not to notice; Zé Pedro suppresses a smirk)

Jean Pierre: One of these additional horsemen was there to lead the way. As you can imagine, the roads in those days were not always clearly marked. They did not always have a map, and there was no GPS... The Dutch had not invented the Tom Tom yet...

(Jean Pierre smiles at Jan Kees, who pretends to be humbly embarrassed, but feels secretly proud)

Jean Pierre: So one of the riders would ride ahead, making sure they were still on the right way. His job was simply to show the way, or "to lead the way". This role was named by the English as "leader".

Heinz: OK, good. Anything else?

Jean Pierre: I just want to emphasize that the term "leadership" is actually a distortion, because there was never such a word in French... This is something that the Americans created after the war, but it doesn't make sense, in terms of the concept. I will stop here because Joe is getting angry, so we can discuss this later when everyone has spoken.

Heinz: *Gut!* Mr. Peartree, you may speak now.

Joe: Well, like I said, leadership is about action. When people are kind of lost, a leader is someone who will take charge of the situation, make a decision and lead the team out of the woods, to victory! A leader will not only show the way out, he will also be the example, the role model for what needs to be done! He will be brave, and focused, and committed to results. 'Cause in the end, it's the results that count, and a leader will drive the team to overcome obstacles and achieve the target, get the results and win!

Jean Pierre: Does all that come with Sylvester Stallone, with Bruce Willis or with both?...

Heinz: Please, Mr. Poireau, allow him to finish.

Joe: I'm through. Next guy.

Heinz: That would be you, Meneer Peerboom.

Jan Kees: I've already spoken. Zé Pedro is next.

Heinz: Please, Mr. Pereira. What are your ideas about leadership?

Zé Pedro: Well, I started by asking all of you to help me... I guess I think that a leader is someone who should take responsibility for the team, show the way they should go, but also make sure that they are all following him, and that they continue to work as a team. I mean, if people start scattering along the way, then that leader is not a good leader. He has to keep the team together, and they should trust each other and trust him as a leader. There needs to be trust before they can follow him anywhere, and the leader also needs to be respected and followed.

Heinz: *Gut!* Anything else?

Zé Pedro: No, *tudo bem*, that's all for now. So tell us, Herr Birnbaum, what is your expert opinion on this?

Heinz: (clears throat, sits up straight) Leadership can be very simple, as long as there is a structure and a process in place. The leader should be an expert in the subject at hand, but if he is not, then he needs to listen to the experts and subsequently make an informed decision. That is all there is to it!

Zé Pedro: Thank you all for your input. Who wants another beer?

Jean Pierre: I think I'll have a *Cognac* instead...

Joe: Bourbon for me. On the rocks.

Jan Kees: I'll have a *wittebier* this time.

Heinz: I will have a *schnapps*!

Hu Tan: Maybe I will have any beer made by Inbev... a Budweiser, Stella Artois, Brahma, Beck's, Leffe...

Zé Pedro: Why does it have to be made by Inbev?

Hu Tan: We are buying the company, so I might as well taste one of their products...

25. Graduation Speech

It's that time of the year again, when millions of students in the Northern Hemisphere are graduating from High School or from College, and the ceremonies that celebrate this rite of passage typically include speeches by invited figures, whose mission it is to articulate the rejoice of communities involved and to dispense advice for the future. I've just been through the process of attending such ceremonies once again (I have four daughters, two of them already graduated from College, one from High School, and one to go).

Most of the speeches I have listened to or read in the media are quite inspiring and offer true moral value to youngsters and older people alike. They sort of reinforce our collective ethics and express the hope that the next generations will carry on the values that have shaped our culture, perhaps developing them further and creating a better world for generations to come. There are, unfortunately, a few of these graduation speeches that are just a lot of rubbish, really.

By that I mean that there are some myths in our world, which are precisely the notions that make this world a shameful place to be in, which make this world in such terrible need of improvement. These myths are precisely what we all, and especially the younger generation, need to fight against in order to make this a better world. Hearing these myths once again exalted makes me quite upset, and urges me to lash out against these attempts to perpetuate them during these rites of passage. These are crucible moments, in which graduating youngsters should be spared from hearing advice most likely to lead them to maintain a status quo that demands changing.

So here are a few myth-busting comments I would like to make, in order to help graduates to make their own judgment about some of the stuff they are exposed to at these ceremonies. Please forgive my eventual lack of moderation. I am exaggerating to provide some balance against the myth-perpetuating statements I've heard.

Myth-Busters

Typically in many speeches you hear the exaltation of Focus, Discipline, Hard Work. People tell you to study very hard and to develop your Willpower and Rational abilities. I have to say that these notions are, at best, heavily biased by a cultural perspective, which includes a tendency to think that there is "only one way to do things right", and tries to impose that perspective upon the whole planet, even by force. Examples of that are the invasions of Iraq and Afghanistan, and the NATO operations in the Balkans, trying to force "democracy" unto people even if they are to be killed in the process. This rubbish needs to be stopped.

Focus can be a good thing, but you can easily get too much of a good thing. It's like "the dark side of The Force", as anyone who is a fan of "Star Wars" (or of "That 70's Show") can tell you. The exaggeration of a virtue quickly becomes a malady and the driver of disaster. Focus becomes narrow-mindedness. It alienates you from your surroundings. It drives environmental recklessness and irresponsibility (as in lack of response-ability, making you unable to respond effectively) regarding what happens around you. Margaret Wheatley points out that animals are not focused. Rather, they are always equally attentive to what they are doing (eating, drinking, hunting, playing, mating, nursing their young) and to what goes on around them. Which is why they are able to escape to safety when their predators (such as "Man") approach them. Animals may dedicate 50% of their attention to one thing, but the other 50% is always dedicated to maintaining their awareness of their surroundings. When we exalt the need to focus we are distancing ourselves from our environment and making ourselves more vulnerable.

I'm not talking just about physical threats or the physical environment. It applies also to interpersonal relationships and to the economy. The investment bankers and traders who created the American mortgage bubble and the global credit crisis were all very focused! They were focused on making money and getting huge bonuses. They lost touch with the impact they would make on the economy and on society as a whole. They did not see the signs of the bubble bursting, though the signs were there. Many people even saw those signs of impending disaster, but chose to ignore them. They were too focused on saving their own assets and "didn't give a chuck" about anybody else.

Therefore, rather advising graduates to "focus", I would rather say, "don't focus!" Never lose your ability to notice what is going on around you. Never lose your awareness of other people and of what they are feeling. Be prepared to drop what you're doing and engage in interaction with somebody else. Jorge Luis Borges told us that on their deathbeds, people do not regret not spending enough time at the office. They do not wish they had had more focus on their careers. Rather, it's the opposite. They regret focusing too much on work, and not dedicating time enough to interacting with the people and the world around them.

Discipline is exalted as a virtue as if enduring pain was a good thing. Self-limitation is a form of discipline, and it is also exalted. We hear that we should avoid the temptation to enjoy life and be free to do what we want. Instead, people are urged to "be disciplined", which means sacrificing your own judgment and feelings on behalf of doing what some lunatic has ordered you to do. It's the justification of all war crimes, from the Nazi concentration camps to the CIA torturing of suspects. Again, the dark side of the force.

If discipline comes from within, rather as engagement instead of commitment (the difference may be subtle but it is very important), then it is a different thing. Engagement stems from inspiration, not from following orders. It originates in passion, in emotions, rather than in obedience to external norms.

Class of 2009 (all of you who are graduating this year, whether from High School or from College), I urge you to be engaged rather than disciplined. Be true to your heart, more than to your mind. Be aware of what you feel as much as of what you think. Decide what path you wish to take, rather than following others blindly. Listen to your body and to your emotions as often as you listen to your mind.

Hard work can be pretty stupid, so it should not be exalted as a value "per se". You can easily get yourself killed and end up bringing death to many people around you, if you simply work hard. Working hard just for the effort is a form of self-punishment. Think about what you're trying to accomplish, rather than just exerting yourself to death. You're not doing penitence. You should be trying to get some result from your work, something that will generate value for others. Work is a means to an end, and the ultimate end is to make this world a better place for those around you. If you consider work as an end in itself, you will just drive yourself crazy, and you'll drive people around you crazy too. Plus, if you're working on the wrong things, you may bring harm to others, rather than benefit. An accidental explosion will get you killed, plus the people around you. It will be like killing your allies with "friendly fire", rather than hitting your targets. A bleak example: more French civilians were killed by Allied "friendly fire" in the Battle of Normandy alone, than there were British civilians killed by German bombing in all of WW II. And they criticize the French for not being grateful...

Smart work is better. Figuring out a better way of doing things is better than just repeating the same way of working, harder and harder. Smart work avoids casualties. And don't forget to dedicate time to love, also.

When asked by a journalist what were the criteria for mental health, Sigmund Freud gave a simple answer: "Loving and working". Healthy people are those capable of loving and working. Expressing care for others and producing something. That's the best advice for graduates: love and work. Personally, I would keep it in that order of importance, though I cannot say whether that was Freud's intention.

Studying hard, to me, is also a myth, supported by the myths of the supremacy of rational thinking and of willpower and discipline. Don't get me wrong; I am not saying that you should not study. What I want to say is that studying, to me, is about learning something that you are interested in learning. You don't need to study "hard". If you are not interested in something, you will not learn it by spending hours on end reading text when you would rather be doing something else. Simply sitting there reciting to yourself will not make you learn anything. Why? Because learning only happens when your emotions are involved. It is not about rationality, it is not about willing yourself into doing something that you are not genuinely interested in, or naturally capable of.

It's more about engagement and talent, rather than willpower and commitment. If you are interested in something, you will learn it regardless of your teacher, no matter how bad he/she is. If you have a good teacher, he/she will allow your interest to arise, rather than attempt to impose "discipline" on you. The best learners are those who are passionate about the subject. That makes it so easy for them to learn it. The trick is to be in touch with your own feelings and senses, to be "whole", rather than being a slave of your rational mind. Then you will discover the things that you are passionate about and you will have great fun learning more and more about them.

Conclusion

Class of 2009, try do discover which is **the way you learn**, as a person. Learning is a unique process for each individual; every person does it in a slightly different way. It involves your emotions more than your rational thinking. It's got more to do with your talent than with your willpower. Get to know yourself (Socrates said that, it's not new). Become "whole", fully aware of what you sense, feel and think. Allow your natural talents to surface. This will help you find your own way. Keep learning. Suffering like a martyr is not a pre-requisite to success or to happiness.

The best graduation speech I've heard this year came from Mr. Tweedie, a High School teacher at the International School of Amsterdam. It was not about "winning", "focus", "discipline" or any of that rubbish. It was about observing toddlers and young children in the playground, from his office window. He saw that sometimes a child would fall from the toys they were playing on, and bruise an arm or scrape a knee. He saw there was always a classmate that would run to them and help them get up from the ground, pat them on the back, comfort and encourage them. This was Mr. Tweedie's advice to the graduates: be there for someone else when they fall down, comfort and encourage them. That will help make this a better world. It was a lesson learned from small children, rather than from some "old fart". I totally agree with his message. I also believe we have much more to learn from our children than from some of our elders.

26. Creating Jobs

Unemployment has remained high in the US and it is even higher in certain parts of Europe, notably in Spain and Portugal. This is all due to the financial meltdown of 2008, which started in America and affected the whole world from Chattanooga to China. In order to create more jobs we must get rid (at least temporarily) of a deeply rooted bias that we all have, in all cultures, in favor of efficiency. Efficiency creates value in the short term, but it destroys value in the long-term, unless we manage it with a long-term perspective. Most organizations and governments, however, are severely lacking in long-term perspective. This does not help job creation.

Barking up the wrong tree

The latest effect of that meltdown is the mistakenly named "Euro crisis", which is actually a power struggle between speculators (investment banks and hedge funds) on one side (who like to refer to themselves as "investors") and the governments of the European Union. As this tug-of-war continues and extends in duration, some speculators make millions; others (like JP Morgan Chase) lose millions. Meanwhile, politicians win or lose elections and millions of people are out of work, in Europe and in the US.

The financial interventions of American and European governments have been mainly unsuccessful (to put it mildly) in solving the global crisis. Some would argue that the remedies used have been worse than the original illness.

Decisions have been made to cut spending as a way to balance government deficits. This has in turn affected growth in a negative way; so that the deficits have increased in relation to shrinking GDPs. Companies have stopped investing, afraid of an uncertain future. The policies of austerity have not recovered confidence in the environment, on the contrary: they have increased the lack of confidence, leading to less investment and less jobs. Everything is going in a downward spiral, which only benefits opposition parties everywhere and traders who thrive on chaos.

Finding the right tree

By accident, I stumbled into a different approach, which might be useful in this context. Like many people on the affluent side of the world, I am trying to take on a healthier life-style. I've discovered that this includes having more physical activity, rather than sitting behind a computer all day and writing stuff like this article... Health specialists say that I should be more active.

Exercising four times a week is not enough, if between these short bursts of activity I remain most of the time sitting behind a desk. Therefore, I started to consciously change my habits in order to get up more often, leave my desk and go to a different part of my house, climbing stairs to different floors, for the simplest of things. For instance, rather than going downstairs to the kitchen and taking a bottle of water back to my desk with me, to drink from it during the next couple of hours, I decided to leave the bottle in the refrigerator. Every time I feel thirsty, I need to get up from my chair, walk downstairs to the kitchen and fill my glass with water, then go back up again to continue writing. After a few minutes my glass is drained and I need to repeat the trip downstairs.

Observing my behavior, my daughter remarked "Dad, why don't you take the bottle of water with you? It's more efficient!" That's when I realized that we all have this bias to be more efficient, to make less effort for our gains. However, when we consciously **want** to make more effort for each gain, because we wish to be more active, we need to fight against the bias towards being efficient.

Creating jobs is easy

... if we really want to! Do we?

The difficulty governments are having makes me wonder whether they really want to create jobs... There are so many interests at stake in these issues that it seems somebody must be benefitting from the high unemployment figures. I can easily spot some obvious beneficiaries:

- opposition parties of current governments
- media pundits who thrive on bad news to sell newspapers and increase their audience on TV

- business people who would like to see their salary costs going down
- speculators who have invested heavily betting on certain currencies going up or down

You may add your own candidates to this list using the space below. Feel free to use extra sheets if the space provided is not enough...

The main obstacle to job creation is not macro-economic, it is much more basic and important than that: it is our cultural bias towards efficiency. We have all learned to seek efficiency since our early childhood. Every baby in every culture wants instant gratification with minimum effort. This part is not cultural, it's human nature.

As we grow older and become toddlers and young children, the cultural aspect, which is learned and not innate, begins to take shape.

Some cultures put a greater value in performance, and reward it more, rather than quality of life and caring for others. This is what Hofstede has researched and identified as the third cultural dimension in his 5 dimensional model of culture values. I often refer to it as "Performance Orientation".

In every culture there is some level of "Performance Orientation". We all strive to perform well, to some degree. What varies is simply how important the culture considers this to be, in situations where a choice is required between performance and quality of life. In some cultures, performance is very important; in others, not so much.

The relevance to job creation is: the more efficient a group of people (or an individual) can be in executing any task, no matter how simple, the less effort is required. When it comes to complex tasks grouped to form jobs, the greater the efficiency, the less effort is required, and the less people are necessary to accomplish the task.

Slobonian lamp changers

Take the old joke about "how many Slobonians does it take to change a lamp?" (Replace "Slobonians" with the favorite nationality you enjoy making fun of).

The classic answer is "Five: one to hold the lamp and four to turn the stool he is standing on!"

We all laugh at this because the situation seems ridiculous.

But wait! Consider this as a metaphor for the economy and the labor market. By using five people to change lamps, we have five people employed. When we choose for efficiency, we use only one person (probably we pick the best performer) and we leave four people looking for a job. That's an 80% unemployment rate!

Most economists will tell you that these four people have actually been "liberated" from doing boring, repetitive work. They should all be happy to now be free to look for more interesting things to do and to "self-actualize" their potential...

Well, guess what? They will not find "more interesting things to do"... They will not find **anything** to do because all organizations are equally seeking efficiency and letting go of excess people, making them "redundant"! When the economy is shrinking, that is a real issue.

The problem is: those four guys become a social liability. Being unemployed is one of the worst things that can happen to anyone. (The problem is not "being fired"; the problem is not being able to find another occupation). In our performance-oriented societies, people feel useless, worthless. Soon these feelings turn into depression and illness; otherwise they turn into anger and rage against the establishment. Our four guys will be joining mobs that go rioting in London, or looting whenever they see a chance to do it. They will turn to crime as a way to feel useful and to be doing something. Nothing is worse than feeling useless.

Meanwhile, our remaining lamp changer has been made redundant too. He has been replaced by a robot, or his job has been off-shored to some place (Mainland Slobonia) where someone else will do it for half the cost.

The economists cheer what has happened. Another worker had been liberated! He can be re-trained to become a web designer or to do some other cool thing.

Guess again: our lamp changer is totally incapable of learning how to do "cool things" like web designing. He is a simple bloke, can barely read, and he enjoys physical tasks like changing lamps. And there are millions of people like him out there.

A different tack

So, what if our main goal was not to be more efficient, perform better, make more money with less effort? What if our main goal (at least temporarily) was to find something productive for those five people to do, so that they would not feel excluded and useless?

This is what job programs should be about. The sad thing is that nothing that I've said is really new.

In his wonderful book "Small Is Beautiful", E. F. Schumacher has argued similar points, as early as 1973. By the way, his book is subtitled "A study of Economics as if people mattered". Yet his ideas were soon forgotten.

There are also other simple mechanisms that have been used (limitedly) in the US in the past, like job sharing. Why are these mechanisms not being used more extensively?

When we look at Europe, we see that unemployment rates are much lower in The Netherlands and in Scandinavia than in other parts of the European Union.

There may be some macro-economic reasons for that, but there is also an important cultural reason: these countries have the lowest performance-orientation scores in the world. One of the consequences of that is that many people (more than in any other part of the world) choose to work fewer hours per day or fewer days per week. They end up exercising a kind of "job sharing", although they do not use that label.

The result is: more people working, feeling included and productive in society, even though performance is not a priority. Social unrest is lower than anywhere else, as are unemployment rates.

The US and the UK, plus Spain and Portugal, could easily create job programs that would allow a lot of people to do a little work and keep them off the streets. Besides "job sharing", working fewer hours or fewer days, there are hundreds of jobs involving simple tasks like sweeping the streets, tending to public parks, loading and unloading, which could employ literally millions of people.

Most of these activities have been mechanized in the past 30 years, in ways that we now take for granted. Forklifts do the loading; trucks with robot arms collect garbage; other trucks with mechanic brooms sweep the streets. All these machines have reduced the number of people employed in those tasks, in order to gain efficiency. Perhaps we need to suspend mechanization and create labor-intensive jobs deliberately, in order to employ more people.

These programs could be temporary, lasting a few years only, and gradually be discontinued as the economy starts growing again. Yet they need "thinking out of the box" from policy makers. They require a real "paradigm shift", away from seeking efficiency and towards putting job creation as our real priority.

27. The Meaning Of Life

Pupil: O Master Khard, I have come a long way on the American Express all the way to Mount Visa in search of the meaning of life. Will you lead me further on this path? Tell me, what is the meaning of life?

Khard: Life is its own meaning.

P: I don't get it...

MK: Not very clarifying, heh? Let's elaborate. The purpose of life is to live. All living beings share that principle, even the often despicable human beings, who have a reputation of selfish destruction of everything around them (including other human beings) as part of their effort to survive, to go on living.

P: Surely there must be something more to this. Why do we live?

MK: Maybe there is no why. Why do you need a "why"? Can you not accept that life is what it is, and try to enjoy it while you can, and fulfill its purpose? Can you not focus on "how", rather than in "why"?

P: OK, let's park the "why" for now and come back to it later. What about the "how"?

MK: The purpose of life is to perpetuate life. The purpose of my life, your life, our lives, is to make this world a better place for everyone to live.

P: OK, then how? How do I make this place a better place?

MK: Love and work. Love yourself. Love your neighbor (but not your neighbor's wife; we come back to that later). Love life itself. Make love (but enjoy responsibly). Make children. That is making more lives and perpetuating life through your descendants.

P: What about gay marriage?

MK: Next best thing. Homosexual love trumps heterosexual hatred, every time. If people found out that Jesus never really had an affair with Mary Magdalene, that he actually had a thing with Judas and later dropped him to hang out with Peter (no wonder Judas felt betrayed), none of this should make a difference regarding his teachings. People should be less uptight about sex. Relax and enjoy it.

P: Sounds fun. What about work?

MK: Work to produce something that will benefit others. Your work is your contribution to the people around you. Combine love and work. This is not about making out at the office. This is about loving your work, loving what you do, doing things as an act of love to promote the life of others. It is also about loving in a productive way. Love should be expressed in a way that helps others, it is also a contribution. Ultimately, love and work may be different facets of the same thing. They are together.

P: What about death?

MK: Shit happens. There are only two things that are certain in life: death and taxes. Sorry, that was a joke for the auditors. Actually taxes are an act of love, they are a contribution to the well-being of the community we live in. But I agree with "The Economist": fiscal policies allow room for improvement. There is much to be improved.

P: You're avoiding the death question...

MK: Death appears to be the end of life, but it is the end of consciousness as we know it in this dimension, or this world. Our body continues to have life within it after our consciousness departs, in the form of bacteria and worms and what we call "decay". They are different forms of life that continue living to consume the body when our "soul" is no longer there.

P: But what happens after death? What happens to the soul?

MK: We don't know. We make assumptions, we make guesses. In fact, we just do not know. And this ignorance about what happens bothers many people, it makes them anxious.

P: What about Heaven and Hell? Don't our souls go to one place or the other?

MK: We don't know. Because we don't know, we invent things to fill in the gap of knowledge. We think: "there must be something", so we imagine a wonderful place that is a reward for everyone who has been "good" and a terrible place that is punishment for everyone who has been "bad". We call those "Heaven" and "Hell" and we make up all kinds of stories about those imaginary places. Some people believe there is a place in between them, where you suffer some punishment, but not forever, and you can eventually make the transition into "Heaven". Some people call that "Purgatory". Others call it "TV summer re-runs".

P: But surely all this must have been created and organized by someone, some "God" who designed the world.

MK: It ain't necessarily so. We do not know. We fill our gap of knowledge, again, by inventing the existence of a "God" or many "Gods". We cannot understand a world that was not created by somebody, so we invent a character. We say that "God created Man in his own image" when it appears to be more the other way around: Man created God in his own image. The fact is that different people believe in different "Gods". Maybe "God" is actually "life", rather than somebody who created life. The fact is that we cannot prove it one way or the other. It is an act of faith, like supporting the New York Mets in American baseball, or supporting Feyenoord in Dutch football. It doesn't make sense, but some people still do it.

P: But what about all those paintings in churches?

MK: That's just the way some people believe that God should be like. In Islam there are no pictures of "God". In Hinduism there are many gods and many pictures. So who is right?

P: Good question. I was about to ask you that question.

MK: They are all right when they choose to believe in that. People who choose to believe that there is no "God" are also right. What is "wrong" is to reject and kill other people just because they believe in something different from what you believe in. Taken to the extreme, we should all be killing each other because we all believe in a "different" God. Faith in God is a very personal experience. Even people going to the same temple, professing the same religion, they have very individual and different interpretations about what "God" is like.

P: I feel like I'm losing my religion...

MK: The fact is that religions are undoubtedly created and developed by people, and most religions are used by people to manipulate other people. Most religions distort the principles set forth by their founders and use the founder's name in vain, just to promote their own agendas. Jesus and Mohammad would be shocked to see the amount of bullshit that goes on today and that is attributed to them. Perhaps the Buddha would be the most shocked, because he was very clear in saying that he had found his own path to enlightenment and he wanted others to learn how to find their own paths, but he specifically asked: "don't turn this into a religion".

P: And they did it anyway.

MK: It just goes to show that you can't ever trust your disciples. Better to get a lawyer to do all your writing for you and a publicist to be your spokesperson. And still they will screw it up, and still people will interpret it in a way that satisfies their needs, regardless of the intended message.

P: So the world is kind of screwed up, huh?

MK: Ask yourself this: are you helping to screw it even more, or are you trying to "unscrew it"? Imagine this huge screw: are you turning it in a way that helps to unscrew life or are you turning it in a way that screws it even more?

P: The screw of life...

MK: Speaking of that, let's get back to "your neighbor's wife".

P: What does she have to do with all this? I swear, I was just trying to borrow a cup of sugar!

MK: I mean, figuratively speaking. Your purpose in life is to love all others and to work making a contribution to all others, and that includes respecting all others too. In practice, life is complicated. Your freedom stops at the limit when you face another's person right to freedom. The interpretation of this is what gets us all into trouble. So many people interpret it in such a way as to authorize them to screw everybody else (in more ways than one). That is why you need the rule of law.

P: Now it's bullshit. Why do you need to bring lawyers into this?

MK: The rule of law means that a group of people agrees on a set of rules they will obey, as guidelines for their behavior. They are interpretations that are meant to make life easier so that you don't need to get into a long philosophical discussion every time you go out to buy bread.

P: I suppose it should make sense, though in practice it often doesn't.

MK: Precisely. Rousseau called that "the Social Pact": everybody gets together and agrees on how we are going to get along, in order to avoid long heated discussions every day. No wonder he was French. The problem is that people easily get caught up in differing interpretations of the laws, whether it's about buying a "baguette" or about invading Iraq. As an overall guideline, we should never forget that our actions should promote life.

P: What about wars?

MK: That's a no-no.

P: Not even Holy Wars?

MK: Especially "Holy Wars". By definition, a war is not holy. To go to war "in God's name" is to negate God, to negate life.

P: What about self-defense? And pre-emptive action?

MK: Does not apply. Christ never said, "Invade Afghanistan!" nor did Muhammad ever say, "Kill those American imperialist bastards". These are all distorted interpretations of what is attributed to the founders of religions. People take things out of context and twist them around. You can find anything in the Bible or in the Qur'an to suit your selfish agenda and justify your purchase of a new Play Station 3, but the fact remains that it is a distortion. Pre-emptive action is very dangerous because you can start imagining all kinds of bad things in your mind about your neighbor, in order to justify shooting him and feeling righteous about it. Anyway, that is why there are tribunals and courts, and international courts and the UN. The purpose is to settle differing interpretations.

P: But the UN doesn't work! It's just a huge bureaucracy! And the legal systems are screwed up everywhere.

MK: Then act to un-screw them. Make changes to the system. Make the UN work. Re-shape the "Social Pact". Ask yourself: am I helping to un-screw things or am I helping to get them more screwed?

P: Some times the only way to change things is through revolution.

MK: You say you want a revolution? Well, you know, we all want to change the world. But when you talk about destruction, don't you know that you can count me out. It can be a peaceful revolution, like Gandhi demonstrated

P: Yeah, I know. You think it's gonna be all right...

MK: In order to defend and promote life, you need to act. But your actions should be about love and work, not about hate and destruction.

P: How come there are so many people in the world involved in wars, hatred and violence? If it was not part of human nature, everybody would live in peace.

MK: Good point. Love and hate, life and death, they are both part of us, like "Yin" and "Yang", like Obama and Cheney. One cannot exist without the other.

P: You mean Obama and Bush.

MK: Bush was just the front man. In order to preserve life, we need to kill. That is the paradox. Every time we eat, we are destroying some form of life, even the vegetarians. We incorporate the life of plants and animals for our own nourishment. This does not give us a license to kill other people for nourishment, nor does it give us license to kill animals for pleasure or sport, nor to destroy forests to make cardboard images of Britney Spears. We need to maintain balance. We are part of the circle of life. We need nourishment, but when we abuse our need, we are no longer promoting the circle of life, we are upsetting it. The balance involved is rather delicate, and people often are not aware of it. That's why it's so easily upset.

P: Yeah, but Man is the higher being in the food chain, so humans get to decide what to eat and what to change in their environment in order to survive.

MK: Careful. Those are very "Northern" concepts. Deep in the Amazon Jungle there are still many tribes that have never had contact with Europeans or Asians. Their culture is still intact. A few years ago a few explorers made contact with some of these tribes and were very careful not to disturb them, unlike previous explorers who either killed the natives, imprisoned them as slaves or, more recently, brainwashed them to behave like "civilized" people. Anyway, this time they just made contact and tried to learn as much as possible from these tribes. And they learned some interesting things.

P: Such as?...

MK: The natives called themselves "Masters of the Universe", though they had never heard of Wall Street. They considered themselves Lords of the Forest, the center of the world. However, they said that with great power comes great responsibility. They sang in groups about how as Lords of the Forest they were charged with maintaining harmony in the forest. They hunted, they fished, they planted and harvested crops. But they did all that in such a way as to maintain the circle of life, to keep the balance. They did not hunt or fish for sport, only for nourishment. They did not take "pre-emptive action" against jaguars or pythons or alligators. They just drove them away from their village. They felt responsibility for keeping balance, not only regarding their interactions with animals, but even regarding interactions among animals and between animals and plants. They realized, for instance, that fruit were there to serve as food also for birds and monkeys, so they had no right to pluck more than their share if it would leave animals wanting. These natives have been true to these principles for centuries, long before ecology was discovered by modern civilizations. We should think twice before we call ourselves "civilized" and before we consider them "primitive". They may be "primitive", but they are not "inferior" to our modern societies.

P: You sound like Greenpeace. Are you a member?

MK: Used to be. Left when they became a corporation. The lesson here is to keep the balance and to remain humble. When we start feeling too cocky, we end up abusing our freedom. The Social Pact needs to be broadened to include other species, respecting their rights and maintaining the balance.

P: Tell me this is not going to end up in a "Global Warming" discussion.

MK: Global Warming is a fact. What is still under discussion is how much of an impact do human beings have on it. Maybe we never did anything to accelerate it, and maybe there is nothing we can do to slow it down. I don't know. What I do know is that, in the past, even the recent past, when people found out that there was something harmful being used (like lead-based paint), initially they were rebuked. Actually, it took years, even decades of discussions before everyone accepted that lead was harmful and stopped using it. There are always people interested in maintaining the status quo for economic reasons. The discussion on the impact of civilization on Global Warming is probably going to take a while, but the concerns about the environment go far beyond global warming. Even if we conclude that humans have no impact on global warming, we should continue to recycle plastic instead of dumping it in the oceans. We should balance our fishing practices, not only because we want to be "nice" to the salmon, but because if we don't, there won't be any salmon left for us to eat! Global Warming is one thing. Balance in the circle of life is another thing, regardless of global warming. We need to recover the balance (it has definitely been upset, nobody denies that) to ensure our long-term survival. Global warming is just one aspect of the picture. Even without global warming, pollution is bad for your health.

P: It's just that it's such a pain to have to recycle, to be careful not to upset the balance... It was so much easier to live carelessly, no worries...

MK: Sure. It was also easy to cross the road without looking, when there were only people and horses going about. The more technology we add to our lifestyles, the more safeguards we need, to maintain the balance and continue promoting life. This is not about stopping progress. It is about ensuring that progress continues to happen in a way that really benefits people, and not only benefits the makers of a hazardous product. For instance, we need to continue traveling and having vacation trips. They promote peace and understanding. If airplanes bring about pollution, then we need to improve the technology so that airplanes no longer cause pollution, but we should not ground all planes or refrain from traveling.

P: Shouldn't we all just negate all worldly pleasures and join a monastery to develop our spirit?

MK: You should, if that's what gets you off. Me, I want to enjoy red wine and chocolate while I am still trapped in this material dimension. I want to do that with balance, until it's time for me to go (either to another dimension or to simply disappear from existence). I want to enjoy life and make it more enjoyable for the people around me and for generations to come. I will not abuse my freedom. I refuse to pay a fortune for a bottle of wine, to me that would be a distortion. But I am quite willing to pay what I consider to be a fair price for good quality wine. Is alcohol bad for your health? Too much of it is bad. A glass or two keeps the balance.

28. The Next 100 Years

George Friedman's Book

Friedman wrote a book with this title at the end of 2008. I have always enjoyed reading the work of "futurists" and I read this with eagerness, thinking it would rank among other greats such as the writings of Alvin Toffler, John Naisbitt, Arthur C. Clarke, Herman Kahn.

What a disappointment! It turns out that Friedman is an "armchair admiral" who bases all his forecasts on geopolitics, a concept that was already deemed outdated by Toffler in "Powershift" (1990), twenty years ago...

How did Friedman's book become a bestseller, then? Quite simply, because it says what a lot of people would like to hear. It caters to everyone who thinks that war is inevitable and even desirable to spur economic growth, regardless of which countries or cultures are involved. A lot of people at the Pentagon must have loved it, plus everyone who makes money from making and selling arms and weapons.

The main predictions that Friedman presents make captivating headlines. They are:

1. The "Muslims vs. Christians/Jews" conflict will fizzle out before 2020, no need to worry about that
2. China will not become a world power, but will be fragmented into smaller countries by 2020
3. Russia will attempt to revive the Soviet Union and will fail, fragmenting again and losing territory to its neighbors
4. The US will engage in World War III against Poland, Japan and Turkey in 2050 (these will be the four major powers in the world by then)
5. World War III will be fought by missiles fired from "battle stars" in space and from secret bases on the dark side of the moon
6. The US will dominate the world throughout all of the 21st Century and will emerge from WWIII even stronger and more dominant

7. Germany and France will slowly lose relevance from 2020 onwards, and South America and Africa will remain irrelevant at least for the next 50 years
8. In 2080 American power will be challenged to war by Mexico (with Brazil as an ally) in an attempt to dominate North America and regain the territory it lost to the Americans in 1848.

The author does some fairly good analysis work. He raises some interesting issues. He tries to spot "underlying trends" which drive his analysis. However, he fails miserably when drawing conclusions, often contradicting his own initial assertions. And the reason for that is that he has some basic assumptions that are quite biased and mistaken. These biases throw his conclusions off track.

Friedman's vision has a strong Anglo-Saxon bias. It comes from a "Contest" culture, in which the underlying values are performance, competing to win, bigger is better, and the use of force is the best way to reach your goals. He makes the basic mistake of assuming that all cultures share these same values. This is a gross mistake. Scandinavians do not think like Americans, neither do the Chinese, the Indians, the Arabs. Not even the Russians think like Americans (this may come as a surprise to some folks at the Pentagon...).

Friedman identifies (correctly) some important social trends, though all of them already widely known and explored in today's media, such as the "graying of the workforce", the decrease in population growth, the increased participation of women in management and politics, the fact that this will impact the structure of the family. In one of the most disappointing features of his book, he fails to take his social analysis further. He fails to predict how the greater presence of women as business and political leaders all over the world might affect diplomacy and mitigate the risk of all-out wars (Sarah Palin excepted). He fails to predict how a population who will be 30 years older on average might affect the way politics are carried out or how that will affect decisions about war.

Friedman also neglects some other very important underlying trends, such as:

1. the inter-connectedness of the new generations: as people all over the world are able to remain connected instantly, 24x7, anywhere, how will that affect people's disposition to go to war? When war victims can broadcast instantly videos of the horrors of war, live to the whole world, how will that affect

the support of such attacks?

2. The increase in travel: as people travel more and more and interact directly with other cultures, wouldn't that make it less likely to "demonize" distant "tribes"? If more Iranians visit the US (and vice-versa), won't that make it evident that Bush and Ahmadinejad had more in common than they had in contrast? (We'd be better off without both of them...)
3. The globalization of business: if one third of assets in the US are actually owned by the Japanese, Turks and Europeans, wouldn't that make them less prone to attacking the US? If American companies have their manufacturing done in Turkey and Poland, how likely are these companies to support bombing their own plants?

Because of his military bias, Friedman fails to see that:

a) generals do not rule the world
b) wars will be fought in very different ways in the future (forget about playing "Star Wars" on the moon...)

Let's take the cynical view that "money makes the world go around". Businessmen rule the world, not generals. Generals are manipulated by businessmen to serve business interests. Businesses elect politicians. Candidates cannot get elected without significant business support, anywhere. When countries go to war, it is because enough businessmen stand behind it. This basically means that there have to be enough businesses involved in selling weapons and war supplies compared to businesses that will make more money if a war is avoided. The trend, therefore, is that poor countries, with low acquisition power, are the ones targeted (Africa, Middle East). The more affluent a country, the more consumers of global products it has, the less interested businesses will be in attacking these consumers, since there will be more money to be made from selling goods to them then from selling weapons to attack them. The game has changed. We're not playing "Battleship" or "Combat"; we're playing "Monopoly".

I won't even go into the moral & ethical aspects of war. Both generals and businessmen tend to consider such aspects as being naïve and unrealistic.

Will everybody be nice to each other in the future? Will the beauty pageant candidates' ideal of "world peace" finally come true? Will we finally have beauty pageant candidates whose IQ will exceed the sum of their body measurements (36+24+36=96)?

I'm afraid the answer to these questions is negative.

Countries (and international businesses) will still compete and fight each other. However, it is very likely that:

1. countries as "nation-states" will have less relevance than today, making way for "regional economic blocks"
2. rather than shooting missiles or laser ray guns at each other, fighting is more likely to take the shape of cyber attacks. The most relevant environment will be "cyberspace", rather than the moon or the seas. Friedman, as a retired naval officer, correctly realized that the seas will be less relevant in war, but he replaced them with outer space in his military thinking. He would do better to focus on "cyberspace" instead.
3. Szun Tzu, the Chinese military genius of another millennium, described "the art of war" as the art of avoiding combat. That is very likely to be the trend (still) in the next 100 years. We are more likely to have economic wars or cold wars, but the likelihood of involving developed societies in combat will be less and less likely.

Aggression is a part of human nature. However, the evolution of mankind has brought about socially smarter ways of expressing aggression, such as competing in sports. War is not only morally wrong, it is also very stupid. Competition and aggression will continue to exist, but they will be more and more about "mind games" which involve subjugating others, rather than physically destroying others.

Perhaps the biggest unanticipated change we will see in the next 100 years will be a shift towards new ways of education and the search for meaning, rather than clinging to superstition/religion and shooting anybody who does not agree with you. But that's another story, to be explored elsewhere and at another time.

The most worrying aspect of Friedman's book is that so many people are still thinking like him. So many people are still looking at reality using a 19th Century perspective, based on nation-states, geopolitics, and "shooting to survive". Unless we decide to make significant investments in education reform, we still run the risk of seeing some of Friedman's deranged predictions come true.

What Next?

I am all in favor of making predictions about the future. I do not believe that "it's hard to tell what's gonna happen next quarter, let alone 100 years from now!" It is always useful to discuss what might happen in the future. It is especially important because such discussions help us shape what is going to happen.

The future is not "something that happens to us". We make things happen. We all live by choice, not by chance, even though we might not always be aware of it. The more aware of it we are, the better prepared we will be to make decisions that shape the future we want for us.

Therefore, I welcome more discussions about the next year, the next decade, the next century. This will help us develop a better world for our children and grandchildren.

29. Crystal Balls

At the beginning of a new year many people enjoy making predictions about what will happen during that year. This includes "futurologists" who make "scientific" analyses of political, economic and sociological trends, and it also includes somewhat "less scientific" experts such as astrologists, soothsayers, palm-readers and crystal-ball gazers.

To speak about the future it does take balls, not necessarily crystal balls... It takes courage to make forecasts and predictions, which might eventually be totally wrong and leave the authors of such forecasts looking pretty stupid.

I will now join these people who have enough balls to make forecasts, and share with you my own predictions for the next five years. This is what I see when I look into my private crystal balls and tune them to 2015.

Europe

The European Union will continue to advance, hesitantly, towards further integration. There will be moves to align fiscal policies, pensions and other economic issues. They will be accomplished through extensive discussions and much haggling, and this will continue to annoy the Americans (most of all) and everyone who would prefer to see a more clear-cut, decisive process. The cultural diversity of Europe will drive the lengthy discussions, the difficulty in quickly reaching a conclusion. At the same time, the need to create regional unity in terms of economic and political issues, while maintaining diversity in terms of culture, is what will ultimately determine what happens.

Slowly the world will understand that globalization (and European regionalization) is desirable and inevitable in terms of economic issues (such as regional currencies) and political structure (such as empowered regional parliaments). This, however, does not mean cultural integration. Culture moves in the opposite direction, towards greater diversity.

Most analysts fail to realize that culture issues are separate from economic issues. This is why Europe will continue to integrate economically and politically, but will continue to diversify and devolve from a cultural point of view. Europe will have eventually (perhaps 50 years from now) a unified economy, unified legislation, unified structures. Yet it will be more culturally diverse than ever and people will strongly identify with their local "grass roots", while feeling "European" at the same time. To feel "European" includes that feeling of identity with your local roots, it includes the rich cultural diversity that is a characteristic of Europe. European identity and local identities are not mutually exclusive concepts.

Globalization

This paradox, between centralization and unification of economic and political mechanisms, while culture values become more diversified and decentralized, has been previously spotted by Alvin Toffler, in the 70's, when he debunked the Orwellian myth of mass production leading to loss of diversity. As pointed out in "Future Shock" and "The Third Wave", new technologies mean that companies can mass-produce with increasing personalization. Customers can order products according to highly individualized specifications. Rather than buying your Ford Model T only in black, modern consumers can choose from a rainbow of colors and also customize everything about the cars they wish to buy, from what kind of motor to what type of cup-holders they prefer. The beauty of modern production techniques is that you are not restricted to three choices of tennis shoe models: there are thousands of possible choices and you can create your own unique model.

As Sumantra Ghoshal pointed out in the 90's, global companies will need to excel simultaneously in three different axis: global efficiency, regional responsiveness, and innovation. The same forces described in his "Ghoshal Matrix" are at play regarding globalization (and European regionalization). To gain efficiency, economic mechanisms such as sharing a common currency, bringing down trade barriers, allowing for free movement of labor across borders, aligning fiscal policies and retirement policies, will need to be put in place. This will continue to happen, first in Europe, and then in other parts of the world. Global unity will eventually happen, not five years from now, but perhaps a hundred years from now.

At the same time, global responsiveness will increase, driving a different set of issues in the opposite direction, towards decentralization and individuation. This will be about culture, values, personalization, identity. Local culture differences will become stronger, and so will the sense of personal identity, and identification with idiosyncratic groups, which might actually not be "local", but will be groups that share specific values though they might be geographically dispersed.

The paradox will be made possible through innovation, the third axis. Technology will make viable the coexistence of global efficiency and local responsiveness. Innovations in communication, connectivity, production, will make many things possible: the personalization of education, the production of customized consumer goods, the polling of opinions, voting on specific issues (not only at elections). We are barely beginning to experience the benefits of this customization trend.

The rise and fall of nation-states

In this process, the concept of "nation-states" will gradually change and become much weaker than it has been in the 20th Century, when it had its peak. Already in the beginning of the 21st Century we can see that-nation states are decreasing in power. When you think about it, nation-states are a fairly recent and short-lived concept. They were invented in the 18th Century and reached their peak around 200 years later, in the late 20th Century, declining afterwards.

By 2015 it will be increasingly clear that nation-states have been caught in the middle of a "scissors" process: centralization of economics and political structures on one hand and decentralization of culture and identification in the other. The paradox will continue to be stretched.

In politics the paradox will be quite evident. On one hand, there will be increased centralization through the formation of regional blocs such as the European Union. The drivers behind that will be the economic issues and a wish to avoid armed conflict. At the same time, new forms of political representation will drive democracy towards greater decentralization. Local representation will gain strength and there will be greater empowerment of local institutions and local control of budget issues wherever that makes economical sense. Scale will still drive certain issues towards centralization (such as building highways and high speed trains), while whenever possible, local residents will decide on local issues (such as parking regulations and noise levels).

Currencies

By 2015 the Euro will not crumble, rather it will become more robust. The Euro will co-exist with the American Dollar, the Chinese Yuan, and a few surviving "exotic currencies" struggling in different corners of the planet. Perhaps we will already have an international "basket of currencies" along the lines of what the Chinese proposed to the IMF in 2009. If not, at least we should be moving in that direction and away from the "currency wars" seen in 2010.

Geopolitics

When applied to geopolitics, the paradox of the Ghoshal Matrix means that we will move from the polarization of the 20th Century (Allies versus Axis, US versus USSR, Capitalism versus Communism) towards multilateralism. By 2015 it will be clear that political and economic issues will be driven by the co-existence of major powers: Europe; the US and its closer allies; China and its closer allies; and a host of "non-aligned" countries such as Brazil, India, Indonesia and others.

It will be interesting to see the impact this will have on American and British diplomacy. Both these cultures are driven by a polarized vision of the world; it is to be expected that dealing with a multilateral world does not come naturally to them, but rather requires greater effort, compared to the Scandinavians and Dutch, for instance.

Democracy will continue to spread by 2015, driven by connectivity. Democracy will be increasingly fractioned into multiple groups, rather than polarized. It will be more nuanced, rather than "black and white".

China will be more democratic than today, more democratic than it has ever been, but still quite different and unique in its culture and political-economic model, further annoying the "Western" media and analysts who would like to see it behave differently. It will continue to grow, perhaps not always at the fantastic rate seen in the past decade, but I don't see China crashing economically, socially or politically.

There will greater democratization of other countries in Asia, Africa and Latin America. However, they will have each their own political model in tune with their cultures. This means, in most cases, very hierarchical structures, whether "right-leaning" or "left-oriented". It also means multiple political parties in each country, rather than the "two-party model" favored in the US and UK.

New models of democratic representation will emerge in the Middle East, in different parts of Africa, in Asia. They will challenge the known models being used in the US and in Europe, relying more heavily on NGOs and other forms of representation such as web-based social networks and mobile phone polling.

Business and Values

By 2012 the global economic recession will be over and recovery will be well on its way. Growth will continue from then on to 2015, driven by continuous demand in the "emerging" economies. Profitability and unemployment will be less of a problem, so companies will return their attention to "the war on talent".

Talented people will put increasing pressure on global businesses to be socially and politically relevant. Companies who do not address these issues will have difficulty in hiring the best and brightest. That will also require managers to address issues about values, political stances and the balance between individual needs and corporate objectives.

People need meaning and a sense of belonging. In past centuries both were provided by religious and political institutions. Increasingly, they will need to be provided by employers, whether private or government-led institutions. As retirement ages are delayed, due to the collapse of pension funds, the generation gap will increase. It will be felt more intensely as the speed of change continues to test human limits to adaptation.

In 2015 "soft" issues such as having meaningful work, corporate social responsibility, sustainability, will all dominate corporate and individual agendas. New labels will replace the existing ones, but the essence of issues will remain the same. What used to be called "citizenship" will be represented by a new set of "buzz words". Whatever the labels in fashion, the issues of meaning and belonging will be the most important ones, underlying all political discussions and determining the outcomes of the "war for talent" in the corporate world.

Connectivity extrapolated will raise new issues. Everyone will be able to talk to everyone, all the time. This will bring about the end of separations we've grown used to: the separation between "life" and "work", so clear in many Northern Hemisphere cultures, will become blurred, as people remain connected to their work while commuting, while at home, while on holidays. And people will remain connected with their leisure activities while at work, frustrating corporate attempts to stop people from doing that. Most Southern Hemisphere cultures are better equipped to deal with this, since they already have less of a separation between work and leisure today.

Another separation that will fade pertains to geography: it's easy today for people to ignore what is going on in Africa if they live in a different continent. As connectivity continues to increase, no one will be able to say, "that is not my problem, I don't live there". Issues will come to you, wherever you are, whenever you are. We've had glimpses of that with live broadcasts from the Iraq invasion, from the protests in Cairo, and the conversations going on between all parties involved, through twitter and Facebook. This changes the face of war and of social interaction. Would World War II have happened if people had then the connectivity they will have in 2015? Probably not.

Leading and managing people will be changed forever because of connectivity, both in the private sectors and in the public sectors. We should start thinking about this and preparing for it.

Before I bust my (crystal) balls, let me stop here for the time being. There is someone ringing at my door that I had not foreseen would come to see me today...

References

Barnes, Peter – "The Ruling Class", London: Bloomsbury Methuen Drama, 1989

Deutscher, Guy – "Through the Looking Glass - Why the World Looks Different in Other Languages" ,London: Picador, 2011)

Freud, Sigmund – "The Interpretation of Dreams", New York: Avon Books, 1965

Friedman, George – "The Next 100 Years", New York: Anchor Books, 2009

Ghoshal, Sumantra – "Transnational Management", New York: McGraw Hill, 1992

Hofstede, Geert et al. – "Cultures and Organizations" New York: McGraw-Hill, 2010

Kets De Vries, Manfred – "Organizations on the Couch", London: Jossey Bass, 1991

Lanzer, Fernando – "Cruzando culturas sem ser atropelado", São Paulo: Évora, 2013

Schumacher, E. F. – "Small Is Beautiful – A study of Economics as if people mattered", New York: Harper & Row, 1975

Toffler, Alvin – "Powershift: Knowledge, Wealth and Violence at the Edge of the 21st Century", New York: Bantam, 1990.

Toffler, Alvin – "Future Shock", New York: Random House, 1970

Toffler, Alvin – "The Third Wave", New York: Morrow, 1980

Wursten, Huib & Lanzer, Fernando – "The EU: the third great European cultural contribution to the world", article available at www.itim.org

About the author

Fernando Lanzer started as a consultant over 30 years ago, but got sucked into one of his clients and became an HR Manager in a bank. Unable to find a real job, he was stuck in HR and in banks for three decades. During that period he worked mostly in Amsterdam and in São Paulo, where a series of bank acquisitions left him with 23,000 reasons for an ulcer.

Since 2003 he has been living in The Netherlands, where he completed 15 years working for ABN AMRO until being kicked back into consulting.

Fernando travels frequently to different parts of the world helping companies to cope with people issues in change processes, especially regarding cross-cultural differences, organization development and leadership development. He is also a member of the Supervisory Group of AIESEC International, the world's largest student exchange network.

He enjoys red wine, coaching, writing, watching films, facilitating workshops, listening to music and public speaking.

He can be reached at:

www.LCOpartners.com
Fernando@LCOpartners.com
Fernandolanzer.com

www.ingramcontent.com/pod-product-compliance
Lightning Source LLC
Chambersburg PA
CBHW061506180526
45171CB00001B/60
9781480054776